Pam's Kitchen

Recipes for Children
from the YTV Show "Take Part"

Pam Collacott

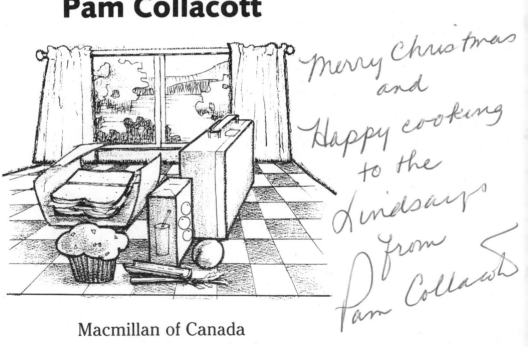

*Merry Christmas
and
Happy cooking
to the
Lindsays
from
Pam Collacott*

Macmillan of Canada

A Division of Canada Publishing Corporation

Toronto, Ontario, Canada

Canadian Cataloguing in Publication Data
Collacott, Pam, 1947-
Pam's kitchen
ISBN 0-7715-9960-9
1. Cookery—Juvenile literature.   I. Title.
TX652.5.C64   1990   j641.5'123
C90-093370-4

1 2 3 4 5   JD 94 93 92 91 90

Cover design by David Montle
Cover photo by Garry Carter
Illustrations by Jean Galt

Macmillan of Canada
A Division of Canada Publishing Corporation
Toronto, Ontario, Canada

Contents

Introduction

Hello! Welcome to my kitchen!

Cooking is lots of fun and a rewarding pastime. Good cooking skills allow you to create delicious foods that you can share proudly with your friends and family. You can make your own snacks and meals, so that you don't have to call a grown-up every time you are hungry. Cooking skills are useful throughout your entire life. And best of all, you get to eat the yummy results of your hard work!

All of the recipes in this cookbook were developed for "Take Part," a children's television show that appears weekdays on the YTV network across Canada. The show stars Lois and Herb Walker and features creative ideas for kids, parents, and teachers. When Lois was looking for someone to cook on "Take Part" a few years ago, I was recommended to her by a person who attended my cooking school in North Gower, Ontario. Over the past four years, I have appeared in 130 cooking segments on "Take Part." In the earlier shows, the cooking segments were called "Super Snacks." Recently, the name has been changed to "Pam's Kitchen."

My mother gave me my first cookbook when I was very young, and my lifelong love affair with cooking began. Teaching children to cook has been an important and enjoyable part of my whole career. Besides showing how much fun cooking can be, I try to emphasize the importance of proper technique and good nutrition. The recipes prepared on "Take Part" by me and my friends Claire, Andrew, Lisa, Sean, André, Megan, Fiona, Matthew, Christina, and Melissa are fast, easy and suitable for children to make by themselves, or with an adult's help.

The most recent segments of "Pam's Kitchen" were taped in my home. We could tell which recipes were the most popular by how fast the crew and children dashed onto the set at the end of each segment to grab a sample of what we had made! During the taping days, family meals consisted mainly of leftovers from the shows. Everyone, including my husband, Read, and my children, Amy and Brian, had a good time. I am grateful for my family's patience then, and all the times they've acted as "guinea pigs" when I've needed to test new recipes!

I hope that you will enjoy preparing the recipes in this book. To make the most of your cooking experience, there are a few important things to remember:

- Always ask permission before you begin to cook. Make sure an adult knows what you are cooking and what ingredients and equipment you plan to use. You should always have an adult's help when you are using sharp knives, food processors, blenders, the stove, oven, or microwave. At the beginning of recipes that use any of these items or that involve difficult preparation steps, I have written *adult help*. You should not attempt these recipes by yourself. When a recipe says *adult supervision* at the beginning, it means an adult should be nearby in case you need help or advice. Remember, all beginning cooks need some help!

- Wash your hands well with soap before you start to cook. If you lick your fingers while you are cooking (and who doesn't?), wash your hands again. Wear clothing you can easily wash and use an apron if possible.

- Read through the entire recipe before you begin, then gather up everything you need (food and utensils) before you start to cook. It's frustrating to get halfway through a recipe and find that you are missing a key ingredient!

- Measure ingredients carefully for best results. Use see-through plastic or glass measuring cups for liquids so that you can get an accurate eye-level measure. Use plastic or metal measuring cups for dry ingredients such as flour or sugar, so you can level off the excess using a straight knife blade or spatula. Plastic or metal cups should also be used to measure fats such as butter or shortening. Press the fat firmly into the cup to eliminate air spaces. Never mix imperial and metric measurements. Use one or the other.

- When you measure in imperial, you will need to know these measurement abbreviations: tsp. — teaspoon; tbsp. — tablespoon. There are 3 tsp. in 1 tbsp., so mixing them up will make a big difference!

- Follow instructions carefully and always combine ingredients in the order given in the recipe.

- Be aware of all the safety precautions you must take in the kitchen. See the Safety Checklist below.

- You will be invited back for more fun in the kitchen if you leave the kitchen as tidy as you found it.

Safety Checklist

Are you a responsible cook? Follow these safety guidelines:

- Handle sharp knives carefully and always cut on a cutting board, not on the counter surface.

- Use oven mitts or pot holders when handling dishes, pans, or plates in the oven or microwave.

- Make sure that electric cords are not hanging over the edge of the counter or over a stove burner.

- Turn pot handles toward the centre of the stove, otherwise you may knock the pot off the burner when you walk by.

- Use dry hands to plug or unplug electrical appliances, or you could receive a dangerous shock.

- Wipe up spills on counters or the floor as soon as they occur. The spills will be harder to clean up later, and a slippery floor can be dangerous.

- Roll up your sleeves, especially if they are large and loose, or change into clothing that won't interfere with your cooking. Clothing should always be inflammable (check with an adult).

- Always turn off the burners and oven when you are finished cooking.

Now you are ready to begin. Take the time to make your food look attractive before you serve it, because food that looks good seems to taste better. Most of all, have a good time in the kitchen!

1
Breakfast Brighteners

Cinnamon Pinwheels

(adult help)

Enjoy these spicy pastries warm with a big cup of hot chocolate.

Ingredients needed:

	1 pkg. refrigerated crescent rolls	
	flour	
2 tbsp.	butter or margarine	25 mL
½ cup	brown sugar	125 mL
½ tsp.	cinnamon	2 mL
2 tbsp.	raisins or chopped candied cherries (optional)	25 mL

Utensils needed:

rolling pin

measuring cups and spoons

small saucepan

pastry brush or table knife

small bowl

sharp knife and cutting board

cookie sheet, lightly greased

metal spatula

How to prepare:

1. Roll dough on a lightly floured surface into a rectangle ¼-inch (6 mm) thick. If the seams of the crescent rolls open up, pinch them back together. Melt butter in saucepan, then brush or spread over the entire surface of the dough.
2. Mix brown sugar and cinnamon together in a small bowl. Sprinkle evenly over the surface of the dough. Sprinkle with raisins or chopped candied cherries if desired.
3. Beginning at one of the long edges, roll up the dough tightly like a jelly roll. Cut into twelve ½-inch (1 cm) slices and place, cut side up, on the prepared cookie sheet, leaving 1 inch (2 cm) between pieces.
4. Bake in a preheated 375°F (190°C) oven for 12 minutes, or until rolls are slightly brown. Cool slightly, then remove from cookie sheet using a metal spatula. Eat warm or at room temperature.

Makes 12 cinnamon pinwheels.

Oatmeal Mini Pancakes

You can tell your friends you ate 20 pancakes—you don't have to tell them they were minis!

Ingredients needed:

¾ cup	oatmeal	175 mL
1¼ cups	milk	300 mL
½ cup	flour	125 mL
1 tsp.	brown sugar	5 mL
¼ tsp.	salt	1 mL
½ tsp.	cinnamon	2 mL
1½ tsp.	baking powder	7 mL
	1 egg, beaten	
2 tbsp.	oil	25 mL
1 tbsp.	shortening	15 mL
	syrup, jam, or applesauce	

Utensils needed:

measuring cups and spoons
small bowl
large mixing bowl and spoon
skillet
metal spatula

(adult help)

How to prepare:

1. Combine oatmeal and milk in a small bowl and let stand for 10 minutes.
2. In a large mixing bowl combine flour, brown sugar, salt, cinnamon, and baking powder. Add egg, oil, and oatmeal mixture and mix well.
3. Melt shortening in skillet over medium heat. When hot, drop small spoonfuls of batter into skillet, leaving a bit of space between pancakes. Cook until tops are no longer shiny, bubbles have formed on the surface, and the edges of the pancakes are dry. Turn pancakes over and cook briefly on the other side.
4. Serve mini pancakes with syrup, jam, or applesauce for breakfast, lunch, or dinner.

Makes 4 servings.

Butterfly Pancakes

(adult help)

These tasty "insects" disappear so fast, they seem to fly away!

Ingredients needed:

1¼ cups	flour	300 mL
2¼ tsp.	baking powder	10 mL
¼ tsp.	salt	1 mL
2 tbsp.	sugar	25 mL
	1 egg	
1¼ cups	milk	300 mL
3 tbsp.	butter or margarine	50 mL
1 tbsp.	shortening	15 mL
	6 cooked sausages	
	applesauce	
	syrup	

Utensils needed:

measuring cups and spoons

small and medium mixing bowls

small saucepan   small skillet

spoon or whisk   serving plate

large skillet   table knife

metal spatula   spoon

How to prepare:

1. Combine flour, baking powder, salt, and sugar in medium-sized mixing bowl.
2. In small mixing bowl, combine egg and milk.
3. Melt butter or margarine in a small saucepan. Add egg mixture to flour mixture along with melted butter or margarine and whisk until smooth.
4. Put shortening into large skillet and place on burner over medium heat.
5. When shortening has melted over the entire surface and the skillet is hot, scoop ⅓ cup (75 mL) of batter into skillet. Cook until bubbles form on the top of the pancake and the edges appear dry, then flip the pancake and cook the other side.
6. Place the sausages in a small skillet and cook over medium heat for 15 minutes, or until the sausages are golden brown. Turn them several times during cooking.

7. To make the butterfly: Place a sausage on a serving plate. Cut the pancake in half and place rounded edges of pancake so they touch the sausage on the plate, to form the butterfly's wings. A spoonful of applesauce forms the butterfly's head. Serve with applesauce or syrup.

Makes about 6 butterflies.

Pancake Initials

Make your initials or, if you're really hungry, make your whole name!

Ingredients needed:

1¼ cups	flour	300 mL
2¼ tsp.	baking powder	10 mL
¼ tsp.	salt	1 mL
2 tbsp.	sugar	25 mL
	1 egg	
1¼	milk	300 mL
3 tbsp.	butter or margarine	50 mL
1 tbsp.	shortening	15 mL
	syrup, jam, or applesauce	

Utensils needed:

measuring cups and spoons

medium mixing bowl

small mixing bowl

spoon or whisk

small saucepan

large skillet

funnel

metal spatula

(adult help)

How to prepare:

1. Combine flour, baking powder, salt, and sugar in medium-sized mixing bowl.
2. In small mixing bowl, combine egg and milk, then add to flour mixture.
3. Melt butter or margarine in saucepan, add to flour mixture, and whisk until smooth.
4. Put shortening into skillet and place on burner over medium heat.
5. When shortening has melted and covers entire surface, you are ready to begin. With an adult's help, hold the funnel 2 inches (5 cm) above the skillet and spoon ¼ cup (50 mL) batter into the funnel. Move the funnel so that the batter forms the letter you want. Make another letter if there is room in the skillet. The letters may be as large or as small as you like.
6. The initial pancakes are ready to turn over when the tops are no longer shiny and are covered with bubbles and when the edges are dry. Turn them over carefully and cook on the

other side for a brief time. Repeat the procedure until all the batter is used up.

7. Serve pancakes with syrup, jam, applesauce, or your favourite topping.

Makes about 12 letters.

• •

Microwave Oatmeal

(adult help)

If you like oatmeal, you'll love this speedy microwave version. There's no sticky pot to clean after!

Ingredients needed:

⅓ cup	quick-cooking oatmeal	75 mL
¾ cup	water	175 mL
	milk, brown sugar, or honey	

Optional ingredients:

raisins, chopped dried apricots, chopped apple, cinnamon, or coconut

Utensils needed:

measuring cups

microwave-safe cereal bowl

spoon

oven mitts

How to prepare:

1. Measure oatmeal and water into a cereal bowl. Stir to mix.
2. Microwave on High for 1½ to 2 minutes, or until the surface of the oatmeal is bubbly all over. Use oven mitts to remove the bowl from the microwave—it will be quite hot.
3. Serve oatmeal with milk and brown sugar or honey, or any of the optional ingredients you choose. Remember to wash fresh fruit toppings before eating.

Makes 1 serving.

Cinnamon Toast

Cinnamon toast is a super snack any time —enjoy it with cold milk in the summer and hot chocolate in the winter.

Ingredients needed:

¼ cup	sugar	50 mL
1 tsp.	cinnamon	5 mL

1 slice bread
per serving

butter or margarine

Utensils needed:

measuring cups and spoons

small bowl and spoon

small funnel

empty spice bottle with shaker top

toaster

table knife

serving plate

(adult supervision)

How to prepare:

1. To make Cinnamon Sugar: Mix sugar and cinnamon in a small bowl. Use a funnel to pour this mixture into the spice bottle. Attach the shaker top.
2. Toast bread in toaster, then spread butter or margarine on hot toast. Sprinkle buttered toast with cinnamon sugar. Cut in half and place on serving plate. Serve immediately.

Makes 1 serving.

Raspberry French Toast

(adult help)

I think this type of French toast tastes just like a jelly doughnut!

Ingredients needed:

	4 slices French bread, 1-inch (2 cm) thick	
	raspberry jam	
	2 eggs	
½ cup	milk	125 mL
½ tsp.	vanilla	2 mL
¼ cup	butter	50 mL
	icing sugar	

Utensils needed:

cutting board and bread knife

table knife

small mixing bowl

fork or whisk

measuring cups and spoons

table knife

pie plate or other flat dish

skillet

metal spatula

serving plate

spoon

small sieve

How to prepare:

1. With an adult's help, cut the bread slices almost all the way through, keeping one side of the crust intact. The bread slice can then be opened like a book. Open the bread and spread raspberry jam in the centre. Close the "pocket."
2. In small bowl, beat the eggs, then add milk and vanilla. Stir with a fork or whisk. Pour this mixture into the pie plate.
3. Melt the butter in the skillet over medium heat.
4. When the butter has melted and covers the surface, dip both sides of the bread slices into the egg mixture, then place slices in the skillet. Cook until first side is golden, then turn over with a spatula and cook until the other side is golden.
5. Place cooked slices on a serving plate. Spoon a small amount of icing sugar into the sieve and shake the sieve over the French toast to dust it lightly with sugar. Serve at once.

Makes 4 servings.

15

Egg in a Ham Cup

Make this for breakfast or lunch to surprise your family. Don't forget to pierce the yolk if you are cooking it in the microwave, or it will explode and make a mess.

Ingredients needed:

1 thin slice of ham

1 egg

pepper

1 tsp.   grated cheese   5 mL

1 slice buttered toast

Utensils needed:

1 small microwave-safe dish or a metal muffin pan

small dish

toothpick

plastic wrap (microwave-safe)

grater

measuring spoons

serving plate

(adult help)

How to prepare:

1. Press the ham slice into the dish or into an indentation of the muffin pan so it forms a cup. Break the egg into a small dish, check for shell bits, then carefully pour it into the ham cup.
2. Microwave method: Sprinkle the egg lightly with pepper. Use a toothpick to pierce holes in the yolk and white of the egg to keep it from exploding in the microwave. Cover the dish with plastic wrap, leaving a small opening for steam to escape. Microwave on Medium for 1 to 1½ minutes, or until the egg white appears to be almost set. Grate cheese. Sprinkle cheese over the egg and let stand for 1 minute before serving.
Regular oven method: Grate cheese, then sprinkle egg with pepper and cheese. Bake in a preheated 400°F (200°C) oven for 6 to 7 minutes, or until egg white is set.
3. To serve: Place the ham and egg cup on a serving plate and accompany with buttered toast.

Makes 1 serving.

Egg in a Hole

(adult help)

More fun than an ordinary egg-and-toast meal!

Ingredients needed:

1 egg

butter or margarine

1 slice of bread

Utensils needed:

small bowl

measuring spoons

small skillet

cutting board and sharp knife

metal spatula

plate

How to prepare:

1. Break egg into small bowl and remove any shell bits. Set aside.
2. Put ½ tsp. (2 mL) butter or margarine in the skillet on a stove burner and turn burner on to medium.
3. Slice bread and butter lightly on both sides, then cut a 2-inch (10 cm) circle out of the centre of the bread.
4. Once the butter in the skillet has melted and covers the surface, place bread in skillet. Carefully pour the egg into the hole in the centre of the bread. Place the bread circle in the pan also. Cook until the egg is almost set, then carefully flip egg and bread over using the spatula. Ask an adult to help you do this. Cook for a minute or two more.
5. Lift egg and bread onto a plate, along with bread circle, and serve at once.

Makes 1 serving.

Homemade Peanut Butter

(adult help)

Mom will like this peanut butter because it has less salt than most commercial brands.

Ingredients needed:

2 cups	shelled roasted peanuts	500 mL
2 tbsp.	vegetable oil (or less)	25 mL

Utensils needed:

measuring cup and spoons

blender or food processor

rubber spatula

small jar or plastic container with lid

How to prepare:

1. Measure the peanuts into the blender or food processor. With an adult's help, turn on the machine and process the nuts until the mixture is smooth. Add oil a few drops at a time if necessary, to make the peanut butter smooth.
2. Use a spatula to scrape the peanut butter into a container. Cover and store in a cool place.

Makes 1 cup.

Strawberry Butter

A special-occasion spread for toast, muffins, or biscuits.

Ingredients needed:

¼ cup	frozen strawberries, thawed and drained	50 mL
⅓ cup	soft butter	75 mL
1 tbsp.	icing sugar	15 mL

Utensils needed:

small bowl

wooden spoon

rubber spatula

plastic container with lid

(adult supervision)

How to prepare:

1. In a small mixing bowl, combine strawberries, butter, and icing sugar together with a wooden spoon until well blended.
2. Use the rubber spatula to transfer the Strawberry Butter to a storage container. Cover and store in the refrigerator for up to 3 days.
3. Serve Strawberry Butter on hot toast, English muffins, or biscuits.

Makes ½ cup (125 mL).

VARIATION 1:
Honey Butter

Combine ½ cup (125 mL) soft butter with ¼ cup (50 mL) liquid honey as above. Makes ⅔ cup (150 mL).

VARIATION 2:
Maple Butter

Combine ½ cup (125 mL) soft butter with ¼ cup (50 mL) maple syrup as above. Makes ⅔ cup (150 mL).

Peanut Butter Breakfast Shake

(adult help)

If you don't have time to sit down to breakfast, this shake will give you the nutrients you need to start the day.

Ingredients needed:

1 cup	milk	250 mL
2 tbsp.	peanut butter	30 mL
	1 ice cube	
	1 banana (frozen or fresh)	
	1 carrot, cut in chunks	
1 tsp.	vanilla extract	5 mL
	frozen berries (optional)	

Utensils needed:

measuring cups and spoons

blender or food processor

large drinking glass

How to prepare:

1. Wash carrot and cut into chunks. Measure all ingredients into blender or food processor.
2. With adult help, blend until smooth.

Makes 1 serving.

2
Snacks

Devilled Eggs

Devilled eggs won't get squashed in your lunch if you put two halves back together (to form a whole egg) before wrapping.

Ingredients needed:

	3 hard-cooked eggs	
1 tsp.	minced fresh parsley	5 mL
	3 or 4 lettuce leaves	
1 tsp.	minced onion	5 mL
2 tbsp.	mayonnaise	25 mL
½ tsp.	prepared mustard	2 mL
	dash of salt and pepper	
	paprika	

Utensils needed:

medium saucepan

cutting board and sharp knife

small bowl and fork

measuring spoons

2 small spoons

serving plate

decorating bag

plastic wrap

(adult help)

How to prepare:

1. To hard-cook eggs: Place eggs in a medium saucepan and cover with cold water. Place on stove burner and cook over high heat until the water is boiling. Lower heat to medium and cook for 15 minutes. The water should be simmering, not boiling, during cooking. Place cooked eggs in cold water for 10 minutes before using or refrigerate for future use.
2. Carefully peel eggs and rinse under cold running water to remove all bits of shell. Pat dry.
3. Cut eggs in half lengthwise. Remove yolks and place them in a small bowl. Mash yolks with a fork.
4. Wash parsley, lettuce, and onion. Mince parsley and onion.
5. To yolks, add mayonnaise, mustard, parsley, onion, salt, and pepper and mix together with a fork until well blended.

6. Place whites on a serving plate lined with lettuce leaves. Spoon yolk mixture into whites or use a decorating bag to pipe yolk mixture into the white halves. Sprinkle the tops lightly with paprika.

7. Serve devilled eggs at once, or cover with plastic wrap and refrigerate until serving time.

Makes 6 devilled egg halves.

• •

Mexican Nachos

You may have eaten these in a Mexican restaurant—now you can make your own.

Ingredients needed:

2 cups	grated mild cheddar cheese	500 mL
	1 bag tortilla chips	
½ cup	taco sauce	125 mL

Utensils needed:

grater

measuring cups

microwave-safe plate or cookie sheet

small spoon

serving dish

oven mitts

metal spatula

(adult help)

How to prepare:

1. Grate cheese.
2. Spread tortilla chips in an even layer on the plate (for microwave) or the cookie sheet (for regular oven). Sprinkle evenly with grated cheese. Using a small spoon, splash taco sauce over the chips and cheese.
3. Microwave method: Cook on High for 1 minute, or until the cheese is melted and bubbly.
   Regular oven method: Broil until the cheese is melted and bubbly.
4. Carefully transfer the nachos to a serving dish using a metal spatula, and serve at once.

Makes 6 to 8 servings.

Cheesy Ham Kabobs

Serve with a whole wheat roll for a yummy snack or a quick meal.

Ingredients needed:

> 4 cherry tomatoes
>
> 8 1-inch (2.5 cm) cubes of ham or other meat
>
> 8 1-inch (2.5 cm) cubes of your favourite cheese
>
> 8 pickle chunks or olives
>
> 4 whole wheat rolls or slices of bread

Utensils needed:

> sharp knife and cutting board
>
> 4 wooden skewers
>
> serving plate

(adult help)

How to prepare:

1. Wash cherry tomatoes and pat dry.
2. Cube ham or meat, and cheese. Slice pickles.
3. Arrange meat and cheese cubes, pickles or olives, and cherry tomatoes on skewers in an attractive pattern.
4. Serve on plates with whole wheat rolls or bread.

Makes 4 servings.

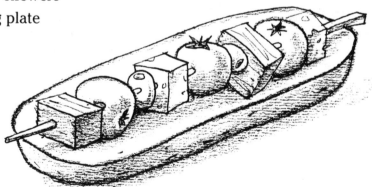

Salami Wedges

These striped snacks are perfect for company.

Ingredients needed:

1 lettuce leaf

parsley and cherry tomatoes to garnish (optional)

4 thin slices salami

3 thin slices of your favourite cheese

Utensils needed:

cutting board and sharp knife

toothpicks

serving plate

(adult help)

How to prepare:

1. Wash lettuce leaf, parsley, and cherry tomatoes, and pat dry.
2. Cut salami and cheese into thin slices.
3. Stack salami and cheese slices alternately, beginning and ending with a slice of salami.
4. Place the stack on a cutting board and stick 6 to 8 toothpicks through the stack from top to bottom, in a circle around the edge (like candles on a birthday cake). Trim off any cheese that is sticking out around the edges.
5. Cut into wedges between the toothpicks and arrange attractively on the lettuce leaf on the serving plate. If you wish, garnish with parsley and cherry tomatoes.

Makes 1 or 2 servings.

Cheese and Apple "Sandwich"

(adult help)

A crunchy "sandwich" made without bread!

Ingredients needed:

>1 apple, cored
>
>3 or 4 slices of cheese
>
>crackers or a whole wheat roll

Utensils needed:

>sharp knife and cutting board
>
>toothpicks
>
>serving plate

How to prepare:

1. Wash apple. Ask an adult to help you remove the core from the apple.
2. Cut apple horizontally into several round slices (each slice will have a hole in the middle where the core was removed).
3. Put the apple back together with a cheese slice between each apple slice. Stick 4 toothpicks through all layers from top to bottom. Cut the apple into 4 wedges with a toothpick in each wedge.
4. Serve with crackers or a whole wheat roll.

Makes 1 large or 2 small servings.

26

Stuffed Apple Wedges

Cinnamon and raisins blended with cream cheese provide a perfect flavour contrast to the crunchy apple.

Ingredients needed:

	1 apple	
¼ cup	softened cream cheese	50 mL
1 tbsp.	raisins	15 mL
	dash of cinnamon	
	brown sugar to taste, if needed	

Utensils needed.

small bowl and wooden spoon
measuring cup and spoons
table knife
plastic wrap
sharp knife and cutting board
serving plate

(adult help)

How to prepare:

1. Wash apple. Ask an adult to help you remove the core from the apple.
2. Put cream cheese in a small bowl and beat with wooden spoon until soft and smooth. Stir in raisins and cinnamon. Add brown sugar if desired.
3. Use a table knife to stuff the centre of the apple with the cream cheese mixture. Cover with plastic wrap and chill for 1 hour, or until cold and firm.
4. With a sharp knife, cut apple into wedges and arrange, skin side down, on a serving plate. Serve at once.

Makes 1 to 2 servings.

Cheese and Cracker Melts

Mix and match the crackers and cheese you use in this recipe.

Ingredients needed:

>8 small, thin slices of cheese
>Sliced olives or pickles
>8 crisp wheat crackers

Utensils needed:

>cutting board and sharp knife
>microwave-safe plate or cookie sheet
>serving plate

(adult help)

How to prepare:

1. Slice cheese, pickles, and olives.
2. Top each cracker with a cheese slice and one or two pieces of pickle or olive.
3. Microwave method: Place crackers on plate and microwave on High for 30 seconds to 1½ minutes, or until cheese is bubbly.
   Regular oven method: Place crackers on cookie sheet. With an adult's help, broil for 1 to 2 minutes, or until cheese is bubbly.
4. Cool slightly before transferring to a serving plate and eating.

Makes 8 servings.

Fancy Cheese Snacks

Surprise your friends with this different version of cheese and crackers.

Ingredients needed:

Crackers or slices of cucumber or zucchini

Several thin slices of your favourite cheese

Garnishes: chopped parsley, diced red pepper, sliced pickles, or pimento-stuffed olives

Utensils needed:

cutting board and sharp knife

small cookie cutters

serving plate

(adult help)

How to prepare:

1. Wash and pat dry any vegetables you are using.
2. Slice cheese, and cucumber and zucchini (if using).
3. With the cookie cutters, cut out fancy shapes in the cheese slices. Put the cheese shapes on crackers or vegetable slices.
4. Use your imagination to decorate your creations using whatever garnishes are available.
5. Put on a serving plate and serve at once, or cover and refrigerate until it's time to eat.
6. Put leftover cheese trimmings and garnishes in small plastic bags and place in the refrigerator or freezer to use in other recipes.

Snappy Cheese Sticks

(adult help)

These cheese sticks taste terrific warm, so make them ahead and reheat at serving time.

Ingredients needed:

½ cup	grated sharp cheddar cheese	125 mL
1 cup	biscuit mix	250 mL
⅓ cup	milk	75 mL
	flour	
2 tbsp.	soft butter or margarine	25 mL

Utensils needed:

grater

medium mixing bowl and fork

rolling pin

measuring cups and spoons

table knife

sharp knife or pizza cutter, and cutting board

greased cookie sheet

How to prepare:

1. Grate cheese.
2. Combine biscuit mix and milk in mixing bowl and stir with a fork until well blended. Roll out on a lightly floured surface to form a rectangle. With table knife, spread with butter or margarine and sprinkle grated cheese evenly over the entire surface. Roll up like a jelly roll.
3. Fold the roll in half, flatten slightly with your hands, then roll into a rectangle ¼-inch (.5 cm) thick. Cut into narrow strips and twist each strip as you place it on the greased cookie sheet.
4. Bake at 450°F (230°C) for 6 to 8 minutes, or until puffed and golden. Serve warm as a snack, with soup for lunch, or instead of rolls with dinner.

Makes 12 to 15 servings.

Ham and Cheese Roll-ups

Pretty little party snacks to share with family and friends. My mother always makes these at Christmas time.

Ingredients needed:

12 gherkins

⅓ cup   cream cheese or   75 mL processed cheese spread, softened

1 to 2 tsp.   pickle juice   5 to 10 mL (from the gherkin jar)

4 thin slices of ham

Utensils needed:

paper towel

small bowl

measuring cup and spoons

spoon

table knife or small spatula

plastic wrap

sharp knife and cutting board

serving plate

(adult help)

How to prepare:

1. Put gherkins on a paper towel and pat dry.
2. In a small bowl, mix together the cheese and enough pickle juice to make the mixture smooth and easy to spread.
3. Completely cover each ham slice with ¼ of the cheese mixture.
4. Place 2 or 3 gherkins along one of the short edges of the ham. Roll the ham around the gherkin, like a jelly roll. Wrap the ham rolls in plastic wrap and refrigerate until cold.
5. Slice each ham roll into 5 or 6 pieces and place on the serving plate, cut side up.

Makes 4 rolls.

Pizza Potato Skins

(adult help)

A great-tasting snack, and good for you too.

Ingredients needed:

	1 baked potato	
1 tbsp.	tomato sauce or ketchup	15 mL
	oregano, garlic salt, and pepper	
½ to 1 cup	grated mozzarella cheese	125 to 250 mL

Utensils needed:

fork

cutting board and sharp knife

2 spoons

microwave-safe plate or baking dish

measuring cups

How to prepare:

1. To bake potato: Prick the skin of the potato several times with a fork. Microwave method: Cook on High for 3 to 5 minutes, or until the potato is tender all the way through when you pierce it with a fork or a sharp knife. Regular oven method: Bake potato in regular oven at 450°F (230°C) for 40 minutes, or until tender.
2. When potato is cool enough to handle, cut in half lengthwise. Use a spoon to scoop out most of the pulp, leaving about ¼ inch (.5 cm) of potato in the shell.
3. Cut each potato shell into 4 long strips and place on microwave-safe plate or baking dish. Spread each strip with tomato sauce or ketchup and sprinkle lightly with oregano, garlic salt, and pepper. Top with as much mozzarella cheese as you like.
4. Microwave method: Cook on High for 1 to 2 minutes, or until cheese melts. Regular oven method: Broil for 2 to 3 minutes, or until cheese melts.

Makes 1 to 2 servings.

Quesadilla
(Mexican cheese crisp)

(adult help)

My son Brian likes to snack on these after school.

Ingredients needed:

1 cup   grated cheddar or   250 mL
             Monterey Jack cheese

1 large flour tortilla

taco sauce,
commercial or homemade

Utensils needed:

grater

measuring cup

paper or microwave-safe plate,
or cookie sheet

metal spatula

cutting board and pizza cutter
or sharp knife

oven mitts

small bowl and serving plate

How to prepare:

1. Grate cheese.
2. Place tortilla on paper or microwave-safe plate (for microwave) or on a cookie sheet (for regular oven). Sprinkle cheese on the tortilla.
3. Microwave method: Cook on High for 1 to 2 minutes, or until cheese melts. Regular oven method: Broil for 2 to 4 minutes, or until cheese is bubbling.
4. Lift tortilla onto cutting board and cut into wedges.
5. Place a small bowl of taco sauce in the centre of the serving dish and arrange the tortilla wedges around the sauce. Dip each wedge into sauce, then munch!

Makes 1 serving.

Cucumber Bites

Like cheese and crackers without the cracker, these taste and look great, and they're fun to make.

Ingredients needed:

½ English cucumber

¼ cup	softened cream cheese	50 mL
1 tbsp.	plain yogurt	15 mL
⅛ tsp.	pepper	.5 mL
	olives, pickles, or parsley	

Utensils needed:

cutting board and sharp knife

serving plate

measuring cup and spoons

small mixing bowl and spoon

decorating bag (optional)

(adult help)

How to prepare:

1. Wash, then thinly slice cucumber and arrange slices on a serving plate.
2. Mix cream cheese, yogurt, and pepper together in a small bowl. Spread the mixture onto the cucumber slices, or spoon into a decorating bag and pipe onto cucumber slices.
3. Cut olives or pickles into thin slices. Top each cucumber slice with a piece of pickle or olive, or with a tiny sprig of parsley (wash first).

Makes about 15 slices.

Well-Dressed Celery

(adult help)

Use different ingredients and your imagination to create a new snack each time you make this recipe.

Ingredients needed:

celery sticks

softened cream cheese, peanut butter, or processed cheese spread

Garnishes: raisins, peanuts, chopped pickles, jam or jelly, banana slices, coconut, sunflower seeds, Cheerios, chopped dried fruit such as apricots, chopped ham or other cold cooked meat, sesame seeds, granola

Utensils needed:

sharp knife and cutting board

table knife

serving plate

How to prepare:

1. Prepare celery: wash thoroughly, trim top and bottom with sharp knife.
2. Fill celery sticks with either cream cheese, peanut butter, or cheese spread using table knife.
3. Sprinkle filled celery sticks with one or several of the garnishes listed (wash fruit first) or with other garnishes of your choice.

Makes 2 or 3 sticks per serving.

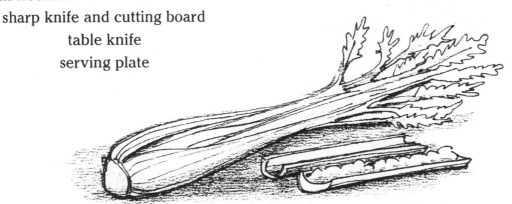

35

Garlic Bread

Make this for your family the next time you have spaghetti for dinner.

Ingredients needed:

	1 unsliced loaf of French or Italian bread	
⅓ cup	soft butter or margarine	75 mL
½ to 1 tsp.	garlic salt	2 to 5 mL

Utensils needed:

bread knife and cutting board

measuring cup and spoons

small bowl and wooden spoon

table knife

long piece of aluminum foil

oven mitts

serving basket and serviette

(adult help)

How to prepare:

1. Using the bread knife, cut the bread diagonally at 1½-inch (3 cm) intervals, not quite through to the bottom of the bread.
2. Mix butter or margarine and garlic salt in a small bowl with the wooden spoon. With table knife, spread one side of each slice of bread with a thin coating of the garlic mixture.
3. Wrap the bread well in foil. Heat in a 300°F (150°C) oven for 20 minutes. Remove from oven using oven mitts. Unwrap and serve warm in a basket lined with a serviette.

3
Dips

Vegetable Dip

This dip also tastes great with potato chips.

Ingredients needed:

1 cup	sour cream	250 mL
1 cup	plain yogurt	250 mL

1 package onion soup mix

raw vegetable sticks
to dip

Utensils needed:

medium mixing bowl

spoon

measuring cups

plastic wrap

cutting board and sharp knife

vegetable peeler

serving bowl and plate or tray

(adult help)

How to prepare:

1. In mixing bowl, stir together the sour cream, yogurt, and onion soup mix. Cover with plastic wrap and refrigerate for 1 hour to blend flavours.
2. Wash the vegetables, peel if necessary, and cut into bite-sized pieces. Refrigerate until serving time.
3. At serving time, pour the onion dip into the serving bowl and place bowl on plate or tray. Arrange dipping vegetables on the plate and serve at once.

Makes 2 cups (500 mL) of dip.

Mexican Bean Dip

When we were taping the first cooking series for "Take Part," the crew liked this dip best of all.

Ingredients needed:

	1 can refried beans	
½ cup	softened cream cheese	125 mL
1 tsp.	chili powder (or less)	5 mL
½ tsp.	onion salt	2 mL
¼ tsp.	garlic salt	1 mL
	tortilla chips	
	celery sticks	

Utensils needed:

can opener
measuring cup and spoons
mixing bowl and wooden spoon
serving bowl and tray
cutting board and sharp knife

(adult help)

How to prepare:

1. Combine beans, cream cheese, chili powder, onion salt, and garlic salt in mixing bowl. Stir until well mixed.
2. Place bean dip in serving bowl and place on tray. Fill the tray with tortilla chips and celery sticks (wash first and trim) to dip. Serve at once.

Makes 6 to 8 appetizer servings.

VARIATION:
Mexican Bean Dip can also be served hot. Heat in a small saucepan over low heat, or in a microwave-safe casserole in the microwave on High for 1 to 3 minutes. Stir once or twice during cooking.

Peanut Butter Dip

Another yummy dip for vegetables, but even better with fruit.

Ingredients needed:

½ cup	finely grated carrot	125 mL
½ cup	crunchy peanut butter	125 mL
¼ cup	orange juice	50 mL

bite-sized raw vegetable pieces to dip

apple or pear wedges to dip

Utensils needed:

vegetable peeler

grater

measuring cups

small bowl and spoon

rubber spatula

serving plate and small dish

plastic wrap

cutting board and sharp knife

(adult help)

How to prepare:

1. Wash carrot, peel and grate.
2. In a small bowl, mix together the peanut butter, grated carrot, and orange juice. Place this mixture in the small dish, cover with plastic wrap, and refrigerate until cold.
3. At serving time, place the bowl of dip in the centre of the serving plate. Arrange the prepared (washed and sliced) vegetable and fruit pieces on the plate around the dip. Serve at once.

Makes about 1¼ cups (300 mL) of dip.

Dippy Snow Peas

Other raw vegetables can be served in place of the snow peas in this recipe.

Ingredients needed:

	20 snow peas	
½ cup	plain yogurt	125 mL
2 tsp.	minced fresh parsley	10 mL
1 tsp.	minced onion	5 mL
⅛ tsp.	garlic salt	.5 mL
⅛ tsp.	pepper	.5 mL
⅛ tsp.	paprika	.5 mL

Utensils needed:

paper towels
measuring cup and spoon
small mixing bowl and spoon
cutting board and sharp knife
plastic wrap
small serving bowl and plate

(adult help)

How to prepare:

1. Wash snow peas and drain on paper towels. Set aside.
2. Measure yogurt into mixing bowl. Wash, mince, and measure parsley and onion, then stir into yogurt. Add garlic salt, pepper, and paprika and stir well. Cover with plastic wrap and refrigerate until serving time.
3. To serve, spoon the dip into a small serving bowl and set in the middle of a small serving plate. Arrange snow peas (and other vegetable sticks if you wish) in a spoke pattern around the dip. Garnish the dip with a small shake of paprika and serve at once.

Makes ½ cup (125 mL) of dip.

Confetti Dip

The colourful vegetable pieces in this dip will remind you of the paper confetti thrown at brides and grooms at weddings. Chop the vegetables for the dip as finely as possible.

Ingredients needed:

½ cup	plain yogurt	125 mL
¼ cup	mayonnaise	50 mL
¼ cup	finely chopped red and green pepper	50 mL
¼ cup	finely chopped carrot	50 mL
2 tbsp.	finely chopped parsley	25 mL
¼ tsp.	garlic salt	1 mL
¼ tsp.	pepper	1 mL
	bite-sized raw vegetables to dip	

Utensils needed:

measuring cups and spoons
medium mixing bowl and spoon
cutting board and sharp knife
serving plate and small bowl
plastic wrap

(adult help)

How to prepare:

1. Measure yogurt and mayonnaise into mixing bowl and stir well.
2. Wash peppers, carrot, and parsley. Chop finely, then stir into yogurt mixture.
3. Add garlic salt and pepper and stir until well mixed. Taste and add more seasonings if needed.
4. Wash the dipping vegetables and cut into sticks or bite-sized chunks and arrange them on the serving plate. Place the small bowl in the centre of the plate and fill with dip. Serve at once, or cover with plastic wrap and refrigerate until serving time.

Makes 1¼ cups (300 mL) of dip.

4
Light Meals and Sandwiches

Mini Pizzas

Good for a snack or a meal. Let everyone choose a different topping for custom-made pizzas.

Ingredients needed:

4 tbsp.	tomato sauce	50 mL

4 small unbaked pizza shells

dash of garlic salt, pepper, and oregano

Toppings: mozzarella cheese, sliced pepperoni, sliced mushrooms, sliced green pepper, chopped cooked ham, drained pineapple chunks, or whatever you like on pizza

Utensils needed:

table knife

measuring spoons

cutting board and sharp knife

cookie sheet

oven mitts

(adult help)

How to prepare:

1. Spread ¼ of the tomato sauce on each pizza shell. Sprinkle lightly with garlic salt, pepper, and oregano. Arrange the toppings you have chosen on the pizzas. Remember to wash all vegetables first. Let each person prepare his or her own pizza.
2. Place pizzas on cookie sheet. Bake in a preheated 425°F (220°C) oven for 10 to 15 minutes, or until the cheese is bubbling. Use oven mitts to remove from oven.

Makes 4 servings.

Happy Pizzas

A yummy pizza that smiles back at you!

Ingredients needed:

2 English muffins, split in half

4 tsp.   tomato sauce or   20 mL
          ketchup

oregano, garlic salt, and pepper

4 slices mozzarella cheese

Toppings: sliced pepperoni or ham, sliced mushrooms, chopped green pepper, drained pineapple chunks, or whatever you like on pizza

Utensils needed:

cutting board and sharp knife

table knife

measuring spoons

3-inch (8 cm) round cookie cutter

cookie sheet or microwave-safe plate

(adult help)

How to prepare:

1. Spread each muffin half with tomato sauce or ketchup, then sprinkle lightly with oregano, garlic salt, and pepper. Add the toppings of your choice. Remember to wash the vegetable toppings first.
2. Use the cookie cutter to cut the mozzarella into a circle the size of the muffin. With a sharp knife, cut a happy face in the cheese. Place a cheese slice on top of each prepared muffin, then carefully place the muffins on the cookie sheet (for regular oven) or plate (for microwave).
3. Regular oven method: Bake in a preheated 425°F or (220°C) oven for 8 to 10 minutes, or until cheese is melted.
   Microwave method: Cook 1 at a time on High for 30 seconds to 1 minute, or until the pizza is hot and the cheese is melted.
4. Serve hot.

Makes 4 servings.

Grilled Cheese Raisin Bread Sandwich

(adult help)

Ordinary grilled cheese never tasted so sweet!

Ingredients needed:

soft butter or margarine

2 slices raisin bread

1 slice cheese, or enough for 1 sandwich

Utensils needed:

table knife

small skillet and metal spatula

serving plate

How to prepare:

1. Butter one side of each slice of raisin bread. Put sandwich together so that the cheese is on the inside and the buttered side of the bread is on the outside.
2. Heat the skillet over medium heat for 5 minutes. Carefully place the sandwich into the hot pan and cook for 3 minutes, or until the bottom of the sandwich is toasted and brown. Carefully flip the sandwich over and continue to cook until the other side of the sandwich is toasted.
3. Lift sandwich onto a plate and cut in quarters to serve.

Makes 1 serving.

Three-Decker Sandwich

Big enough to share with a friend!

Ingredients needed:

3 slices bread

soft butter or margarine

mustard, ketchup, or mayonnaise

1 slice ham or other deli meat

1 lettuce leaf

1 slice cheese

1 tomato

Utensils needed:

toaster (optional)

table knife

cutting board and sharp knife

4 toothpicks

serving plate

(adult help)

How to prepare:

1. If you prefer, toast bread before assembling sandwich.
2. Butter one side of each bread or toast slice, then spread with mustard, ketchup, or mayonnaise, if you wish. Slice cheese and (washed) tomato.
3. Place ham slice and (washed) lettuce leaf on first slice of bread. Top with second slice of bread, then add cheese slice and a layer of tomato. Top with the third bread slice.
4. Stick a toothpick through the entire sandwich near each corner of the bread. Cut the sandwich diagonally into quarters. Arrange quarters, cut side up, on a serving plate. Serve with celery and carrot sticks which you have first washed and trimmed.

Makes 1 big sandwich.

Jelly-Roll Sandwiches

(adult help)

These little sandwiches taste as good as they look. Make one kind or try them all. You need only a little of each ingredient.

Ingredients needed:

5 slices bread

smooth or crunchy peanut butter

½ banana

sweet gherkins

cheese spread or cream cheese

raspberry jam

egg salad (your favourite recipe)

parsley to garnish

Utensils needed:

cutting board and sharp knife

rolling pin

table knife

toothpicks

plastic wrap

serving dish

How to prepare:

1. Cut crusts off the bread slices. Flatten each piece slightly with the rolling pin.
2. First roll: Slice banana thinly. Spread peanut butter on one bread slice and top with banana slices. Roll up and secure with toothpicks. Wrap and refrigerate.
3. Second roll: Spread one bread slice with peanut butter and put a row of gherkins along one edge. Roll up with the gherkins in the centre. Secure with toothpicks, wrap and refrigerate.
4. Third roll: Spread one bread slice with cheese and put a row of gherkins along one edge. Roll up and secure with toothpicks. Wrap and refrigerate.
5. Fourth roll: Spread bread slice with raspberry jam. Put a row of thin banana slices along one edge, roll up and finish as above.
6. Fifth roll: Spread bread slice with a thin layer of egg salad. Put a row of gherkins along one edge and roll as above.

7. To serve: Slice each roll into 5 or 6 pinwheel slices. Arrange attractively on a serving plate and garnish with washed parsley.

Makes 5 small servings.

. . . .

Fun with Peanut Butter Sandwiches

Put veggies and fruit in the sandwich instead of on a plate, and you've got a lunch-on-the-run!

Ingredients needed:

smooth or crunchy peanut butter

4 slices raisin or fruit bread

1 carrot

1 small apple, cored

Utensils needed:

table knife

grater

cutting board and sharp knife

serving plates

(adult help)

How to prepare:

1. Spread a thin layer of peanut butter on each slice of bread.
2. Wash, then grate carrot and sprinkle on one prepared bread slice. Top with a second slice of peanut-buttered bread. Cut into quarters and transfer to a serving plate.
3. For second sandwich, wash apple, core, then cut into thin slices and place all over another slice of peanut-buttered bread. Cover with remaining slice of bread and cut into quarters. Place on serving plate and garnish with any remaining apple slices.

Makes 2 sandwiches.

Pineapple Sandwich Roll

(adult help)

Serve these pretty little sandwiches at your next tea party.

Ingredients needed:

	2 slices of whole wheat bread	
3 tbsp.	softened cream cheese	50 mL
2 tbsp.	drained chopped pineapple	25 mL

Utensils needed:

cutting board and sharp knife

rolling pin

small mixing bowl and spoon

table knife

serving plate

How to prepare:

1. Cut crusts off the bread slices. Flatten each piece slightly with the rolling pin.
2. Combine cream cheese and pineapple in bowl and mix well. Spread this mixture evenly on the bread slices. Roll up like a jelly roll.
3. Cut each roll into 4 or 5 slices and place them on a serving plate, cut side up.

Makes 8 to 10 slices.

50

Sandwiches, Scandinavian-Style

Sandwiches in Scandinavia are open-faced, so take extra time to arrange the fillings attractively. Choose flat lettuce leaves to make sandwiches easier to eat.

Ingredients needed:

2 slices rye bread

soft butter or margarine

mustard, ketchup, or mayonnaise

lettuce

Toppings. sliced cold meats, sliced cucumbers, olives or pickles, cheese, red onion rings, sliced hard-cooked egg, other toppings of your choice

Utensils needed:

cutting board and sharp knife

table knife

serving plate or tray

(adult help)

How to prepare:

1. Each sandwich is made with only one slice of bread. Spread with butter, then your choice of mustard, ketchup, or mayonnaise.
2. Wash vegetable toppings of your choice.
3. Place a lettuce leaf on each piece of bread, then add other toppings in an attractive pattern. Arrange sandwiches on a plate or tray and serve at once.

Pita Pocket

A sandwich and a salad all in one.

Ingredients needed:

½ pita bread (regular size)

butter or margarine

mayonnaise or mustard

1 slice ham or other meat

1 slice cheese

2 slices tomato

4 slices cucumber

1 lettuce leaf

alfalfa sprouts

Utensils needed:

cutting board and sharp knife

table knife

serving plate

(adult help)

How to prepare:

1. Cut pita in half. Open along straight cut edge to form a pocket.
2. Spread butter or margarine on one side of the inside of the pocket and mustard or mayonnaise on the other inside surface.
3. Stuff the pocket with sliced meat, cheese, tomato, cucumber, lettuce, and alfalfa sprouts or any other sandwich filling you like. Wash vegetable fillings before using.
4. Place your pita pocket on a plate (say that fast five times!) and munch away.

Makes 1 serving.

Tuna Mini Pitas

Sandwiches made with pita bread are often called pocket sandwiches, because you stuff the fillings into the pita the same way you stuff things into your pockets!

Ingredients needed:

1 can (7 oz/198 g) water-packed tuna, drained

1 stalk of celery, chopped

¼ cup   mayonnaise, or enough to moisten   50 mL

pepper and salt to taste

chopped lettuce (optional)

1 package mini pita breads

Utensils needed:

cutting board and sharp knife

mixing bowl and spoon

measuring cup

serving plate

(adult help)

How to prepare:

1. Wash celery, trim and chop.
2. Combine tuna and celery in a mixing bowl. Add mayonnaise and a dash of pepper and stir until well mixed. Taste and add salt if needed.
3. Wash and finely chop lettuce, if using.
4. Spoon a small scoop of the tuna salad into each pita bread, which you have first cut in half. Add chopped lettuce if desired.

Makes 4 to 6 servings.

Fruit and Veggie Mini Pitas

(adult help)

More pita pockets for stuffing. Add any or all of the fruit and veggies suggested to make a sandwich to suit your taste.

Ingredients needed:

	1 carrot, grated	
	1 stalk celery, finely chopped	
½ cup	smooth or crunchy peanut butter or soft cream cheese	125 mL
¼ cup	raisins	50 mL
1 tbsp.	chopped dates	15 mL
	1 package mini pita breads	

Utensils needed:

grater
cutting board and sharp knife
small mixing bowl and spoon
measuring cups and spoons
table knife
serving plate

How to prepare:

1. Wash carrot and celery. Grate carrot and chop celery fine.
2. Combine peanut butter or cream cheese in mixing bowl with carrot, celery, raisins, and dates. You can leave out one or two of the vegetables or fruits if you like. Stir until well mixed.
3. Spread a small amount of the filling in each pita pocket, then arrange pitas on the serving plate.

Makes 2 servings.

Hot Tuna Subs

I made these subs for my parents for lunch when I was a little girl. It was the first meal I ever cooked.

Ingredients needed:

¼ cup	chopped celery	50 mL
	1 can (7 oz/198 g) tuna, drained	
2 tbsp.	sweet pickle relish	25 mL
⅓ cup	mayonnaise	75 mL
½ cup	cubed cheddar cheese	125 mL
	dash of salt and pepper	
	4 hot dog buns	

Utensils needed:

cutting board and sharp knife
medium mixing bowl and spoon
measuring cups and spoons
foil or 4 paper towels

(adult help)

How to prepare:

1. Wash celery and chop.
2. In a medium-sized bowl, mix together the tuna, celery, relish, and mayonnaise. Cube cheese, add, and stir. Season to taste with salt and pepper.
3. Split buns in half. Spread ¼ of the mixture on each bun half. Close the bun and wrap in foil (for oven) or paper towel (for microwave).
4. Regular oven method: Heat foil-wrapped buns in a preheated 400°F (200°C) oven for 5 minutes, or until cheese melts. Remove from oven using oven mitts.
   Microwave method: Cook paper-towel-wrapped buns one at a time on High for 30 seconds, or until cheese melts.

Makes 4 servings.

Mini Subs

These subs are great for a picnic.

Ingredients needed:

soft butter or margarine

2 hot dog buns or other rolls

mustard, mayonnaise, or ketchup

2 or 3 slices ham, salami,
or other meats or cheese

2 slices tomato

6 thin slices cucumber

1 lettuce leaf

Utensils needed:

table knife

cutting board and sharp knife

2 serving plates

waxed paper

(adult help)

How to prepare:

1. Spread butter or margarine in both buns. Spread with mustard, mayonnaise, or ketchup, whichever you like.
2. Fill rolls with your choice of meats or cheese, tomato, cucumber, and lettuce. Remember to wash and prepare vegetables before using. Put on plates and serve, or wrap in waxed paper and refrigerate until serving time.

Makes 2 servings.

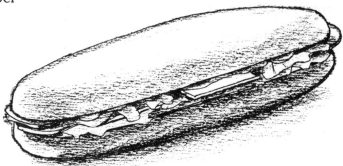

Egg Salad Buns

(adult supervision)

When you pack these buns to take to school, put the egg salad between two layers of lettuce so that the bun doesn't get soggy.

Ingredients needed:

	2 hard-cooked eggs, peeled	
2 tbsp.	mayonnaise	25 mL
1 tsp.	sweet pickle relish	5 mL
	salt and pepper	
	soft butter or margarine	
	2 hot dog buns	
	lettuce leaves	

Utensils needed:

medium mixing bowl
fork
measuring spoons
table knife
serving plate
waxed paper

How to prepare:

1. Put eggs in mixing bowl and mash with a fork until finely chopped. (For instructions on how to hard-cook eggs, see Devilled Eggs recipe in Snack section.) Add mayonnaise and relish and mix well with the fork. Add salt and pepper to taste. Mix again.
2. Spread butter lightly on both sides of the buns. Line buns with (washed) lettuce leaves and spoon in egg salad. Put on a plate and serve, or wrap in waxed paper and refrigerate until serving time.

Makes 2 servings.

Round Hot Dogs

We featured round hot dogs in both cooking series on "Take Part," because the director of the show liked them so much!

Ingredients needed:

1 hot dog

1 hamburger bun

mustard, ketchup, and relish

Utensils needed:

sharp knife and cutting board

microwave-safe plate or small saucepan

tongs

table knife

small serving plate

(adult help)

How to prepare:

1. Using a sharp knife, make small cuts at 1-inch (2 cm) intervals along one side of the hot dog, being careful not to cut all the way through.
2. Microwave method: Place hot dog on microwave-safe plate and cook on High for 30 to 45 seconds, or until the hot dog is cooked and shaped into a round.
   Stove-top method: Place hot dog in small saucepan with enough water to cover the bottom of the pan. Cook over medium heat until the hot dog forms a round, 5 to 8 minutes. Use tongs to remove from water.
3. Place hot dog on bun and garnish with your choice of toppings. Serve on a plate.

Makes 1 serving.

Beanie Weenies

Enjoy these for lunch at home, or when you're on a camping trip or picnic. Cut the hot dog into very tiny chunks for small children.

Ingredients needed:

2 hot dogs

1 can (14 oz/398 mL) baked beans

butter or margarine

whole wheat rolls

celery sticks

Utensils needed:

sharp knife and cutting board

can opener

small saucepan or microwave-safe casserole

wooden spoon

2 or 3 bowls or plates, and forks

(adult help)

How to prepare:

1. Slice the hot dogs into small pieces. Put the beans in the saucepan (for stove-top cooking) or casserole (for microwave) and stir in the hot dog pieces with a wooden spoon.
2. Stove-top method: Cook over medium heat for 8 minutes, or until hot and bubbly. Stir often during cooking. Microwave method: Cover the casserole and microwave on High for 3 to 5 minutes, or until hot and bubbly. Stir once during cooking.
3. Spoon the Beanie Weenies into bowls or plates and serve with buttered whole wheat rolls and (washed) celery sticks.

Makes 2 to 3 servings.

Tuna Cones

If tuna salad isn't your favourite, use chicken salad instead to make these not-sweet treats.

Ingredients needed:

	1 can (7 oz/198 g) tuna, drained	
⅓ cup	chopped celery	75 mL
2 tbsp.	sweet pickle relish	25 mL
⅓ cup	mayonnaise	75 mL
	salt and pepper	
	4 flat-bottomed ice cream cones	
	4 cherry tomatoes, radishes, or pickle slices	

Utensils needed:

sieve

medium mixing bowl

fork and spoon

cutting board and sharp knife

measuring cups and spoons

(adult help)

How to prepare:

1. Place tuna in a sieve and rinse with cold water (this step is not necessary if the tuna is packed in water or broth rather than oil). Drain well.
2. Place drained tuna in mixing bowl and use a fork to break up the large chunks. Wash and chop celery. Add celery, relish, and mayonnaise to tuna and stir with the fork to mix well. Add salt and pepper to taste.
3. Spoon the tuna salad into the ice cream cones and top each cone with a cherry tomato, a radish (wash both first), or a pickle slice.

Makes 4 servings.

5
All Kinds of Salads

Pasta Salad

Change the colour and flavour of this salad by using a different selection of vegetables.

Ingredients needed:

2 cups	cooked macaroni or other small pasta	500 mL
	dash of salt	
½ cup	sliced carrots	125 mL
½ cup	sliced celery	125 mL
¼ cup	sliced radishes	50 mL
2 tbsp.	chopped green pepper	25 mL
	1 green onion, chopped	
⅓ cup	mayonnaise	75 mL
	salt and pepper to taste	
	parsley and paprika to garnish	

Utensils needed:

large saucepan

colander

measuring cups and spoons

sharp knife and cutting board

large mixing bowl

wooden spoon

serving bowl and spoon

plastic wrap

(adult help)

How to prepare:

1. Add uncooked macaroni to a large saucepan of boiling, lightly salted water and cook until tender. Be careful not to overcook. One cup (250 mL) uncooked macaroni makes approximately 2 cups (500 mL) cooked. Drain in a colander.
2. Wash, trim and slice carrots, celery, radishes, green pepper, and onion.
3. In a large mixing bowl, stir together the macaroni and prepared vegetables. Add mayonnaise and stir until well mixed. Add salt and pepper to taste. Stir again.
4. Spoon into a serving bowl and sprinkle the top lightly with paprika. Wash parsley and pat dry. Decorate salad with parsley sprigs.
5. Cover the bowl with plastic wrap and refrigerate until serving time.

Makes 4 servings.

Red and Green Cabbage Salad

(adult help)

A colourful salad to brighten your meal.

Ingredients needed:

3 cups	chopped red cabbage	750 mL
3 cups	chopped green cabbage	750 mL
½ cup	chopped celery	125 mL
	1 apple, peeled, cored, chopped	
½ cup	chopped green pepper	125 mL
	1 carrot, thinly sliced	
½ to 1 cup	mayonnaise or coleslaw dressing	125 to 250 mL

Optional ingredients: sliced radishes, pineapple or orange chunks, chopped onion, raisins, chopped parsley, or chopped sweet pickles

Utensils needed:

cutting board and sharp knife

measuring cups

large mixing bowl

large spoon

serving bowl and spoon

plastic wrap

How to prepare:

1. Ask an adult to cut the cabbages into quarters for you. Wash each section under cold running water. Drain well. Thinly slice one quarter at a time until you have the amount of each kind of cabbage that you need. Mix them together in a large bowl.
2. Wash and prepare the other vegetables and fruit and stir them into the cabbage.
3. Add mayonnaise or coleslaw dressing and stir to mix well. Spoon into a serving bowl. Cover the bowl with plastic wrap and refrigerate until serving time. This salad will keep well in the refrigerator for several days.

Makes 8 servings.

Nutty Coleslaw

Crunchy cabbage salad made even tastier by adding protein-rich peanuts and sweet apple chunks.

Ingredients needed:

6 cups	chopped or grated red or green cabbage	1500 mL
	2 apples, cored, diced	
	1 green pepper, chopped	
⅔ cup	mayonnaise	150 mL
1 tbsp.	sugar	15 mL
1 tbsp.	cider vinegar	15 mL
¼ tsp.	dry mustard	1 mL
⅔ cup	salted peanuts	150 mL

Utensils needed:

sharp knife and cutting board

measuring cups and spoons

large mixing bowl

wooden spoon

small mixing bowl and spoon

plastic wrap

serving bowl and spoon

(adult help)

How to prepare:

1. Prepare cabbage. (See recipe for Red and Green Cabbage Salad for instructions.) Wash and prepare apples and green pepper.
2. In the large mixing bowl, combine cabbage, apples, and green pepper.
3. In the small bowl, combine mayonnaise, sugar, vinegar, and dry mustard. Pour this mixture over the cabbage mixture and stir to mix well. Cover with plastic wrap and refrigerate for 2 hours, or until serving time.
4. At serving time stir in the peanuts and spoon the salad into the serving bowl.

Makes 8 servings.

Fruit Salad with Yogurt and Mint

Make this Greek fruit salad in the summer when fresh mint is growing in your garden, or purchase it fresh from your local greengrocer.

Ingredients needed:

2 ripe bananas, peeled, sliced

2 oranges, peeled, chopped

1 small apple, cored, chopped

2 cups	strawberries	500 mL
½ cup	seedless green grapes	125 mL
¼ cup	sugar	50 mL
1⅓ cups	plain yogurt	325 mL
¼ cup	chopped fresh mint	50 mL

Utensils needed:

sharp knife and cutting board
medium and small mixing bowls
measuring cups
large spoon
serving bowl

(adult help)

How to prepare:

1. Wash and prepare all fruit and combine in medium mixing bowl.
2. Combine sugar, yogurt, and mint (wash and pat dry first) in small mixing bowl. Gently stir the yogurt mixture into the fruit.
3. Spoon into a serving bowl and serve as soon as possible. If you wish, garnish your salad with mint sprigs.

Makes 6 servings.

Jungle Salad

This salad makes me think of the jungle, because so many of the ingredients are tropical.

Ingredients needed:

1 orange, peeled, chopped

1 banana, peeled, sliced

1 pineapple ring, diced

¼ cup	salted peanuts	50 mL
½ cup	fruit-flavoured yogurt	125 mL
¼ cup	flaked coconut	50 mL

Utensils needed:

sharp knife and cutting board

mixing bowl

wooden spoon

measuring cups

serving spoon

2 small serving dishes and spoons

(adult help)

How to prepare:

1. Prepare all fruit as directed above and place in a medium mixing bowl. Stir to mix.
2. Add peanuts and yogurt and mix well.
3. Spoon into serving dishes and sprinkle with coconut. Serve.

Makes 2 servings.

Vegetable Jelly Salad

A sparkling salad to brighten up your meals.

Ingredients needed:

½ cup	peeled, chopped cucumber	125 mL
	1 large carrot, chopped	
½ cup	drained cottage cheese	125 mL
	1 package lime jelly powder, 4-serving size	
2 cups	water	500 mL
	lettuce leaves (optional)	

Utensils needed:

cutting board and sharp knife

medium mixing bowl and spoon

measuring cups

sieve and small bowl

4-cup (1 L) glass measuring cup

1-cup (250 mL) glass measuring cup

small plates or dishes

How to prepare:

1. Wash and prepare vegetables and place in a medium mixing bowl. Drain cottage cheese in sieve set over a small bowl. Add cottage cheese to vegetable mixture.
2. Place jelly powder in 4-cup glass measuring cup, pour in 1 cup (250 mL) boiling water, and stir until crystals dissolve. Pour in 1 cup (250 mL) cold water and stir.
3. Add jelly mixture to vegetable mixture and stir. Refrigerate for ½ hour, or until jelly is partially set. Stir to mix in the vegetables that are floating on the top. Refrigerate 1 to 2 hours more, or until the jelly is completely set. Serve on lettuce leaves on small plates, or in small dishes.

Makes 6 servings.

Jellied Fruit Salad

When my children were very young, they used to make this salad for special dinners when Grandma and Grandpa were visiting. It looks very sparkly and festive.

Ingredients needed:

	1 banana, peeled, sliced	
	1 apple, cored, chopped	
1 cup	seedless grapes	250 mL
2 cups	water or apple juice	500 mL
	1 package flavoured jelly powder, 4-serving size	
	lettuce leaves	

Utensils needed:

cutting board and sharp knife

medium bowl

1-cup (250 mL) glass measuring cup

small saucepan (for stove-top method)

large glass measuring cup and spoon (for microwave method)

small bowls or plates

(adult help)

How to prepare:

1. Prepare fruits (wash apples and grapes first) and place in a medium bowl. Stir to mix.
2. Boil 1 cup (250 mL) of water or apple juice in a small saucepan on the stove, or in a large glass measuring cup in the microwave. Sprinkle in the jelly powder and stir until the crystals dissolve. Stir in 1 cup (250 mL) of cold water or juice.
3. Pour the jelly mixture over the fruit. Refrigerate for ½ hour, or until the jelly is just beginning to set. Stir to mix in the fruit that is floating on the top. Refrigerate for 1 to 2 hours more, or until the jelly is completely set.
4. Serve the salad in small bowls, or on washed lettuce leaves on small plates.

Makes 4 to 6 servings.

Vegetable Tree

A beautiful, edible centrepiece for your holiday parties. Every year, my son Brian makes a vegetable tree for our Christmas Eve celebration.

Ingredients needed:

Bite-sized raw vegetables,
including any of the following:

broccoli florets

cauliflowerets

radishes

mushrooms

carrot chunks

green pepper chunks

cherry tomatoes

parsley

Utensils needed:

cutting board and sharp knife

styrofoam cone

toothpicks

serving plate

(adult help)

How to prepare:

1. Wash and prepare all vegetables.
2. Start at the bottom of the cone and work your way to the top—attach vegetables on the cone with toothpicks in an attractive and colourful pattern. Fill in gaps with sprigs of parsley.
3. Place your vegetable tree on a serving plate and accompany with your favourite dip. (Be sure to save the cone to use another time.)

Note to Parents: If the child preparing the tree is very young, it is safer to have an adult stick the toothpicks into the cone and the child push the vegetable pieces onto the toothpicks. Older children can stick the toothpicks in by themselves.

Ham and Potato Salad

(adult help)

A delicious main-dish salad that's perfect for picnic lunches or dinners.

Ingredients needed:

2 cups	diced cooked potatoes	500 mL
	2 green onions, chopped	
¼ cup	chopped green pepper	50 mL
1 cup	diced cooked ham	250 mL
	1 hard-cooked egg, peeled, chopped	
½ cup	mayonnaise	125 mL
	salt and pepper to taste	
	paprika	
	2 green pepper rings	

Utensils needed:

potato peeler

sharp knife and cutting board

medium saucepan

colander

measuring cups

large mixing bowl

wooden spoon

serving bowl and spoon

plastic wrap

How to prepare:

1. Wash all vegetables and pat dry.
2. To cook potatoes: Wash and peel potatoes and cut into quarters. Put in a medium saucepan with enough cold water to cover. Add a dash of salt. Bring water to a boil over medium heat and cook until potatoes are tender. Drain potatoes in a colander, then cool.
3. Dice potatoes, green onions, green pepper, ham, and egg and mix in a large bowl. (For instructions on how to hard-cook an egg, see Devilled Eggs recipe in Snack section.) Add mayonnaise and stir to mix well. Add salt and pepper to taste. Stir again.
4. Spoon the salad into a serving bowl. Sprinkle lightly with paprika and garnish with green pepper rings.
5. Cover with plastic wrap and refrigerate until serving time.

Makes 4 servings.

Home Salad Bar

Arrange as many of the following items you have available in large or small dishes (depending on the ingredients). Ask an adult to help you decide how much of each food to put out.

Ingredients needed:

lettuce pieces

chopped tomato

chopped green or red pepper

chopped celery and carrot

chopped green onion

chopped hard-cooked egg

croutons   bacon bits

sesame or sunflower seeds

chopped pickles or olives

chopped pickled beets

cottage cheese

grated cheese

chopped red or green cabbage

your favourite salad dressings

Utensils needed:

cutting board and sharp knife

large serving bowl

small serving bowls for garnishes

spoons (for bowls)

(adult help)

How to prepare:

1. Wash and prepare all vegetables.
2. Place lettuce leaves in large serving bowl.
3. Put garnishes in small bowls, each with its own spoon.
4. Invite your family to help themselves —just like in a restaurant.

Composed Salads   (adult supervision)

The following salads use fruit, vegetables, and other foods arranged in a particular way to form attractive and appetizing pictures that you can eat. You'll have fun making them and even more fun eating them. If you don't have all of the food ingredients called for in the recipes, be creative and substitute what's available in your own cupboards and refrigerator. Always wash vegetables before using.

Little Kid Salad

A cute little kid to make and munch! Use the foods listed in the way described:

> Head: 1 slice of hard-cooked egg
> Body: peach half, rounded-side up
> Skirt (if it's a girl): curly lettuce leaf
> Arms and legs: celery or carrot sticks
> Shoes: 2 raisins (or dates if she or he has big feet!)
> Eyes: 2 raisins
> Buttons: 3 currants or raisins on the peach half
> Mouth: a cherry-slice smile
> Hair: coconut, grated cheese, or grated carrot

Candle Salad

Light up your lunch with this yummy salad. Place a lettuce leaf on the plate, then make the candle in the following way:

> Base of candle: pineapple ring
> Candle: half banana, upright in the pineapple ring with the cut side down
> Flame: 1 dried apricot cut with scissors into the shape of a flame. Secure on top of the candle with a toothpick

Kitten

Place a lettuce leaf on the plate, then shape a flavourful feline in the following way:

> Head: peach half, rounded-side up
> Eyes: 2 raisins
> Nose: 1 cherry half
> Whiskers: 6 straight pretzels or thin carrot sticks
> Ears: triangles of apple, banana, or green pepper

Puppy Dog

This dog has no "bark," but you'll definitely want to take a bite! The puppy's face is seen from the side in this salad. Put a lettuce leaf on the plate, then use the following foods to make your puppy:

Head: 1 canned pear half
Nose: cherry, at the narrow end of the pear
Ear: 1 prune, or a slice of marshmallow
Eye: 1 raisin
Collar: a ring of grapes or mandarin orange segments

Bunny Rabbit

Make this little bunny on a lettuce leaf in the following way:

Body: 1 canned pear half
Nose: cherry, at narrow end of pear
Eyes: 2 raisins, on pear, just above the cherry nose
Ears: 2 almonds, stuck into the pear above the eyes
Tail: a small caulifloweret at the wide end of the pear half

Snaky Salad

This snake isn't scary at all. His carrot and celery body are held together with soft cream cheese or processed cheese spread. Cut a carrot and celery stick into bite-sized chunks. Arrange the chunks on the serving plate in a curved line with a dot of cheese between the chunks to hold the snake together. Let the round end of the carrot be his head. Use raisins for eyes (held in place with cheese) and a piece of red pepper or radish for his tongue. Use a small zucchini in place of the celery, if you wish.

Spider

This little guy wouldn't scare Miss Muffet or anyone else away. Make him on a lettuce leaf in the following way:

Body: ½ tomato, rounded-side up
Eyes: 2 slices of olive or radish
Antennae: 2 thin celery sticks or pieces of green onion
Legs: 8 carrot curls (see recipe for Carrot Curls and Radish Roses in this chapter) or carrot sticks
Mouth: piece of green pepper or a raisin

Mousey

A funny little salad to make and munch. Place a lettuce leaf on a plate and make the mouse in the following way:

Body: 1 canned pear half (narrow end is the head)
Nose: small piece of cherry
Eyes: 2 currants or raisin halves
Ears: 2 marshmallow slices (easily cut with scissors)
Tail: 1 green bean

Italian Vinaigrette

(adult help)

Shake up this tangy dressing and toss it with your favourite salad vegetables.

Ingredients needed:

2 tsp.	minced green onion	10 mL
2 tbsp.	vinegar	25 mL
6 tbsp.	vegetable or olive oil	90 mL
¼ tsp.	salt	1 mL
¼ tsp.	dry mustard	1 mL
¼ tsp.	dried basil	1 mL
	dash of pepper	

Utensils needed:

sharp knife and cutting board

measuring spoons

jar with a tight-fitting lid

How to prepare:

1. Wash, pat dry and mince green onion.
2. Measure all ingredients into the jar. Cover the jar tightly with the lid, and shake to mix well.
3. When you are ready to eat your salad, pour some of the vinaigrette over the salad greens and toss well with salad servers or 2 large spoons. Serve the salad as soon as the vinaigrette is added.
4. If you do not use all of the vinaigrette, store the jar in the refrigerator.

Makes ½ cup (125 mL) dressing.

Carrot Curls and Radish Roses

(adult help)

Use these fancy vegetable garnishes to decorate your salad or sandwich plate.

Ingredients needed:

> 1 or 2 carrots
>
> radishes

Utensils needed:

> cutting board and sharp knife
>
> vegetable peeler
>
> toothpicks
>
> medium mixing bowl half-full of cold water
>
> a few ice cubes

How to prepare:

1. Scrub carrots and radishes and cut off stem ends. Peel the carrots.
2. To make carrot curls, use vegetable peeler to remove long strips from carrot. Roll up these strips and secure with toothpicks. Place in bowl of water with ice cubes. Leave until ready to serve, then drain well, and remove toothpicks.
3. To make radish roses, set the stem end of the radish on the counter. Use a sharp knife to carefully cut 5 or 6 **U**-shaped slits around the sides of each radish from top to bottom, being very careful not to cut these pieces off. When you place the radishes in ice water, the slits will open up like flower petals and the radishes will look like flowers.

Crazy Croutons

A simple way to perk up your lunch.

Ingredients needed:

> several slices of toast
> grated cheese (optional)

Utensils needed:

> tiny cookie cutters
> cutting board

(adult supervision)

How to prepare:

Use the cookie cutters to cut funny shapes out of the toast. Put the crazy croutons in a tossed salad or float in bowls of your favourite soup. If you wish, sprinkle grated cheese on the croutons before using.

6
Desserts

Applesauce Mousse

(adult help)

A light, fluffy dessert that your family will love.

Ingredients needed:

	2 egg whites	
1 cup	smooth applesauce	250 mL
1 tbsp.	icing sugar	15 mL
½ tsp.	lemon zest (grated lemon rind)	2 mL
2 tsp.	finely chopped nuts	10 mL

Utensils needed:

egg separator

measuring cup and spoons

large mixing bowl

zester or grater

electric mixer

rubber spatula

4 small serving bowls

How to prepare:

1. Separate egg whites from yolks using egg separator.
2. Put applesauce, egg whites, and icing sugar in the mixing bowl. Grate lemon rind and add to applesauce mixture. Beat with electric mixer on high speed until light and fluffy.
3. With spatula, scrape into individual servings dishes and sprinkle chopped nuts on top. Serve at once or refrigerate.

Makes 4 servings.

Applesauce

A delicious dessert on its own, applesauce can also be used in cakes or muffins, or it can be served with pancakes, French toast, or pork chops.

Ingredients needed:

	4 apples, peeled, cored, and quartered	
2 tbsp.	water	25 mL
¼ tsp.	cinnamon	1 mL
	sugar to taste, if needed	

Utensils needed:

cutting board and sharp knife

6-cup (1.5 L) glass casserole with lid (for microwave)

plastic wrap (microwave-safe)

medium saucepan (for stove-top method)

fork

potato masher

wooden spoon

measuring spoons

medium bowl

(adult help)

How to prepare:

1. Wash and prepare apples. Place the apple chunks and water in the casserole (for microwave) or saucepan (for stove top).
2. Microwave method: Cover the casserole with lid or plastic wrap. If plastic wrap is used, leave a small opening to allow steam to escape. Microwave on High for 6 to 8 minutes, or until the apples are tender when you pierce them with a fork.
   Stove top method: Place lid on saucepan and cook over medium heat for 10 minutes, or until the apples are tender when you pierce them with a fork.
3. Mash the apples with a fork or a potato masher, then add cinnamon. Taste and add a bit of sugar if needed. Stir well, then transfer applesauce to a bowl, cover with plastic wrap, and refrigerate until cold.

Makes 3 to 4 servings.

Apple Crisp

This delicious dessert is a traditional family favourite.

Ingredients needed:

	6 apples, peeled, cored, sliced	
⅔ cup	brown sugar	150 mL
¼ cup	soft butter or margarine	50 mL
⅓ cup	flour	75 mL
⅓ cup	oatmeal	75 mL
½ tsp.	cinnamon	2 mL
¼ tsp.	nutmeg	1 mL
	vanilla ice cream or sweetened whipped cream (optional)	

Utensils needed:

sharp knife and cutting board

8-inch (20 cm) square baking pan, lightly greased

measuring cups and spoons

small bowl

wooden spoon

fork

(adult help)

How to prepare:

1. Wash and prepare apples and spread slices in lightly greased baking pan.
2. Cream brown sugar and butter together in small bowl using wooden spoon. Add flour, oatmeal, cinnamon, and nutmeg and stir until well mixed and crumbly. Use your (clean) hands for this if you wish.
3. Sprinkle sugar mixture evenly over apples in pan.
4. Regular oven method: Bake in a preheated 350°F (180°C) oven for 30 minutes, or until apples are tender when you pierce them with a fork. Microwave method: Make sure that you use a glass or microwave-safe baking dish. Do Steps 1 to 3 above, then microwave on High for 6 to 10 minutes, or until apples are tender when you pierce them with a fork.
5. Serve warm or cold, with vanilla ice cream or sweetened whipped cream if desired.

Makes 4 servings.

Applesauce Parfait

(adult help)

Use your own homemade applesauce or a commercial brand in this delicious dessert.

Ingredients needed:

1½ cups	applesauce	375 mL
4 cups	vanilla pudding or plain yogurt	1 L
	4 maraschino cherries	

Utensils needed:

measuring cups

4 parfait dishes or dessert bowls

2 spoons

How to prepare:

1. Spoon 2 tbsp. (25 mL) applesauce into the bottom of each dish. Spoon ⅓ cup (75 mL) pudding or yogurt on top of the applesauce. Repeat layers twice more, or until applesauce and pudding or yogurt are all used up.
2. Top each parfait with a cherry and refrigerate until serving time.

Makes 4 servings.

> **VARIATION:**
> Instead of applesauce, you can use chopped peaches, pineapple, bananas, or other fruit of your choice. Remember to wash fruit before using.

Rainbow Jelly Parfaits

(adult help)

These sparkling treats are pretty to look at and fun to eat.

Ingredients needed:

6 cups	water	1.5 L

3 packages jelly powder, 4-serving size, different flavours and colours

Utensils needed:

large glass measuring cup

spoon

1-cup glass measuring cup

6 glasses or parfait dishes

How to prepare:

1. With an adult's help, boil 1 cup (250 mL) water and pour into large measuring cup. Add first package of jelly powder and stir until crystals dissolve. Pour in 1 cup (250 mL) cold water. Pour an equal amount of this mixture into 6 glasses. Place the glasses in the refrigerator for 1 hour or until the jelly is firm.
2. Prepare the second package of jelly powder in the same manner as the first. Slowly pour this flavour over the firm jelly in the glasses. Refrigerate for 1 hour or until firm.
3. Repeat Steps 1 and 2 with the third package. Refrigerate until firm. The Rainbow Jelly is ready to serve as soon as it is completely firm.

Makes 6 servings.

Yogurt Parfait

Make this parfait in a small juice glass if you don't have a parfait glass. Then you will be able to see the pretty layers.

Ingredients needed:

	½ banana, sliced	
¼ cup	graham cracker crumbs	50 mL
1 cup	plain or flavoured yogurt	250 mL

Utensils needed:

knife and cutting board

parfait or juice glass

measuring cups and spoon

long-handled spoon (if using parfait glass)

(adult supervision)

How to prepare:

1. Slice banana. Place 2 or 3 banana slices in the bottom of the parfait or juice glass. Sprinkle 1 tbsp. (15 mL) crumbs over banana. Spoon in ⅓ cup (75 mL) yogurt. Add a few more banana pieces, another tbsp. (15 mL) crumbs, and ⅓ cup (75 mL) yogurt. Repeat layers until yogurt is used up.
2. Top with a sprinkling of crumbs and a banana slice. Serve at once.

Makes 1 serving.

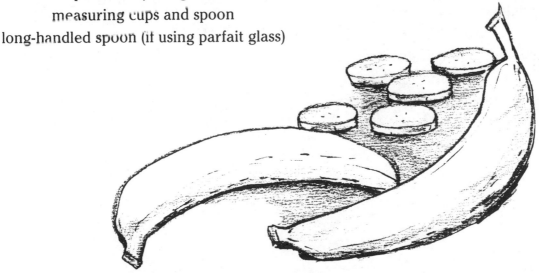

Banana Trifle

This dessert looks best made in a glass bowl so that the jelly roll slices can be seen through the glass.

Ingredients needed:

3 cups	vanilla pudding	750 mL
	1 small raspberry jelly roll	
	2 bananas, sliced	
½ cup	whipping cream, whipped	125 mL
	cherries to garnish	

Utensils needed:

glass serving bowl

measuring cups

sharp knife and cutting board

spoon

electric mixer

small mixing bowl

rubber spatula

plastic wrap

(adult help)

How to prepare:

1. Prepare pudding following package directions.
2. Slice jelly roll into 8 pieces. Slice bananas. Line bottom and sides of the serving bowl with jelly roll slices. Cover with banana slices. Spoon pudding over bananas and smooth the top.
3. Whip cream, then spread on top of pudding, using rubber spatula. Decorate with cherries.
4. Refrigerate, covered with plastic wrap, for at least 1 hour before serving.

Makes 4 servings.

Chocolate Fondue

(adult help)

A special occasion treat—serve it the next time your best friend comes to visit.

How to prepare:

STOVE-TOP METHOD:

Ingredients needed:

6 oz.	package semisweet or milk chocolate chips	175 g
½ cup	corn syrup	125 mL
1 tsp.	vanilla	5 mL

For dipping: orange segments, pineapple chunks, banana chunks, strawberries, apple slices, seedless grapes

Utensils needed:

measuring cup and spoons

double boiler

wooden spoon

serving bowl and tray

rubber spatula

fondue forks

large glass measuring cup or microwave-safe bowl

1. Put 2 cups (500 mL) water in bottom of double boiler and, with an adult's help, set on stove burner over medium heat.
2. In top of double boiler combine chocolate chips, corn syrup, and vanilla. Place on double boiler bottom and heat and stir until chocolate melts and mixture is smooth.
3. Arrange washed and prepared fruit on serving tray, leaving space in the centre for the serving bowl.
4. Transfer chocolate to serving bowl, using rubber spatula to scrape the pan, and set the serving bowl on tray. Pass a fondue fork to each guest. Spear a piece of fruit and dip into chocolate.

MICROWAVE METHOD:

Combine chocolate, corn syrup, and vanilla in a large glass measuring cup or microwave-safe bowl. Microwave on Medium for 2 to 4 minutes, or until melted. Stir every 2 minutes. Continue with Steps 3 and 4 of stove-top method, above.

Makes 4 servings.

Cookies and Cream Dessert

This dessert has been a favourite of mine since I was a little girl. At our house, we sometimes make one large dessert instead of four individual ones and use it as a birthday cake.

Ingredients needed:

1 cup	whipping cream	250 mL
2 tbsp.	sugar	25 mL
	1 box chocolate wafer cookies	

Utensils needed:

electric mixer

mixing bowl

measuring cup and spoons

4 dessert bowls

spoon

plastic wrap

(adult help)

How to prepare:

1. With an adult's help, use electric mixer to whip cream and sugar together until cream is stiffly whipped.
2. Place a chocolate wafer in each dessert bowl. Top each cookie with a spoonful of whipped cream. Put wafers on top of cream, then cream on wafers, and repeat until all wafers are used up. End with a dollop of cream on top. Cover with plastic wrap and refrigerate for at least 4 hours before serving to allow time for the cookies to soften.

Makes 4 servings.

Peaches and Cream Dessert

(adult help)

Smooth and creamy—this dessert is delightful!

Ingredients needed:

	1 package peach jelly powder, 4-serving size	
1 cup	boiling water	250 mL
1¼ cups	vanilla ice cream, softened	300 mL
1 cup	fresh or drained tinned peach slices, chopped	250 mL

Utensils needed:

medium mixing bowl

1-cup glass measuring cup

spoon

cutting board and sharp knife

How to prepare

1. Pour jelly powder and boiling water into mixing bowl and stir until jelly crystals dissolve. Add ice cream and stir until it melts.
2. Stir in peaches. Refrigerate until jelly is set, about 1 hour.

Makes 4 servings.

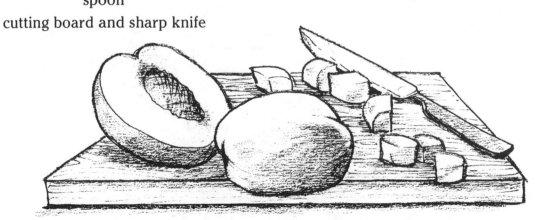

Clown Cupcake Sundae

(adult help)

A party recipe that's as much fun to make as it is to eat.

Ingredients needed:

> 1 cupcake
> 1 scoop ice cream, any flavour
> 2 Lifesavers
> 3 jelly beans
> 1 candy heart
> 1 gumdrop

Utensils needed:

> cutting board and sharp knife
> ice cream scoop
> serving plate

How to prepare:

1. Cut a cone-shaped piece out of the top of the cupcake. This cone will be the clown's hat.
2. Place a big scoop of ice cream in the hole in the cupcake. Use candies to make the face: Lifesaver ears, jelly bean eyes and nose, candy heart mouth, and gumdrop-slice eyebrows.
3. Set the cake-cone hat on the clown's head and serve at once.

Makes 1 serving.

Cupcake Cones

This is a quick treat to make for a large group.

Ingredients needed:

1 single-layer cake mix

18 to 20 flat-bottom ice cream cones

your favourite frosting

candy sprinkles

Utensils needed:

measuring spoons

table knife

cookie sheet or microwave-safe tray

(adult help)

How to prepare:

1. Make up the cake mix according to package directions.
2. Spoon 2 heaping tbsp. (25 mL) of batter into each cone.
3. Regular oven method: Stand the cones on a cookie sheet. With an adult's help, carefully place in a preheated 350°F (180°C) oven. Bake for 20 minutes, or until toothpick inserted into the centre of one cone comes out clean.
Microwave method: Arrange 6 cones in a circle on a tray in the microwave. Microwave on High for 1½ to 3 minutes, or until a toothpick inserted into the centre of one cone comes out clean. Repeat, baking 6 cones at a time, until all cones are baked.
4. Cool cones completely, then frost with your favourite icing. Decorate with candy sprinkles if desired.

Makes 18 to 20 cones.

Wacky Cake

When you read how to put this cake together, you'll wonder how it will ever turn out. It turns out great!

Ingredients needed:

1½ cups	flour	375 mL
3 tbsp.	cocoa	50 mL
1 tsp.	baking soda	5 mL
1 tsp.	baking powder	5 mL
¾ cup	sugar	175 mL
½ tsp.	salt	2 mL
1 tsp.	vanilla	5 mL
1 tbsp.	vinegar	15 mL
5 tbsp.	melted shortening	75 mL
1 cup	warm water	250 mL

Utensils needed:

sieve
8-inch (20 cm) square baking pan
measuring cups and spoons
small saucepan or glass measuring cup
wooden spoon

(adult help)

How to prepare:

1. Place the sieve in the baking pan. Measure the flour, cocoa, baking soda, baking powder, sugar, and salt into the sieve. Shake the sieve gently to sift the ingredients through into the pan.
2. Make 3 holes in the dry mixture. Pour the vanilla into one hole and the vinegar into another. Melt the shortening in the microwave (in a glass measuring cup on High for 1 minute) or in a saucepan on the stove top over low heat, then pour into the third hole.
3. Pour the warm water over all ingredients in the pan, then stir with a wooden spoon to mix well.
4. Bake in a preheated 350°F (180°C) oven for 30 to 40 minutes, or until a toothpick inserted into the centre of the cake comes out clean.

Makes 1 cake.

Lacy Cake Topping

A quick and easy, yet very pretty way, to decorate a cake.

Ingredients needed:

2 tbsp.	icing sugar	25 mL

Utensils needed:

paper doily

small sieve

measuring spoon

(adult supervision)

How to prepare:

1. Just before you are ready to serve dessert, place the doily on top of the cake. Hold the sieve over the cake and spoon icing sugar into the sieve. Shake the sieve gently and stir the icing sugar so that it sprinkles through the holes in the doily and onto the cake.
2. When you are finished, carefully lift off the doily. Be careful not to drop any more icing sugar onto the cake or you'll disturb the pretty pattern you have made.

7
Frozen Treats

Yogurt Popsicles

Use a different juice concentrate each time to create a new flavour.

Ingredients needed:

2 cups	plain yogurt	500 mL

1 can (6 oz/170 mL)
juice or lemonade
concentrate, defrosted

Utensils needed:

can opener

mixing bowl and spoon

popsicle molds or small paper cups
and wooden sticks

(adult supervision)

How to prepare:

1. Combine yogurt and fruit juice concentrate of your choice in a bowl. Do not add water to the concentrate.
2. Pour the yogurt mixture into popsicle molds or small paper cups. Place a stick in the centre and place the molds or cups in the freezer for 2 hours, or until completely frozen.
3. To serve, remove molds by holding them under warm running water for a few seconds, or peel off paper cups.

Makes 4 to 6 popsicles.

Pineapple Yogurt Pops

Not too sweet, but very refreshing.

Ingredients needed:

| ½ cup | plain or flavoured yogurt | 125 mL |
| 2 tbsp. | drained crushed pineapple | 30 mL |

Utensils needed:

measuring cup and spoons

small bowl

spoon

small paper cup and wooden stick or popsicle mold

(adult supervision)

How to prepare:

1. Combine yogurt and pineapple in a small bowl and stir to mix well.
2. Spoon yogurt mixture into the paper cup or popsicle mold. Put the stick into the centre. Place in freezer for 2 hours or until frozen.
3. To serve, peel off paper cup or remove from mold by holding it under warm running water for a few seconds.

Makes 1 to 2 servings.

> VARIATION:
> ## Fruity Yogurt Pops
>
> Combine ½ cup (125 mL) yogurt with 2 to 3 tbsp. (25 to 50 mL) crushed berries, or chopped bananas, peaches, or apricots, and prepare pops as above. Sweeten to taste with honey or sugar if desired. The fruit chunks should be small, as frozen fruit is very icy and hard and large pieces are difficult to eat. Remember to wash fruit before preparing.

Banana Fudge-sicles

A creamy chocolate treat for a warm afternoon.

Ingredients needed:

> 2 bananas, peeled and finely chopped
>
> 1 package instant chocolate pudding mix, 4-serving size

2 cups   cold milk   500 mL

Utensils needed:

> cutting board and knife
>
> measuring cup
>
> medium mixing bowl
>
> wooden spoon
>
> small paper cups and wooden sticks or popsicle molds

(adult supervision)

How to prepare:

1. Chop bananas and set aside.
2. Combine pudding mix and milk in mixing bowl and stir until thick. Stir in bananas.
3. Fill paper cups or popsicle molds with pudding mixture and put a popsicle stick into each one. Freeze until firm, about 2 hours.
4. To serve, peel off paper cups, or remove from molds by holding them under warm running water for a few seconds.

Makes 6 to 8 fudge-sicles

VARIATION 1:

Fudge-sicles

Prepare as above, leaving out bananas.

VARIATION 2:

Frozen Pudding Pops

Create a new frozen treat by using different flavours of pudding. Prepare as above.

Jelly-sicles

These fruity treats are especially nice for very small children because they do not melt and drip as much as regular popsicles.

Ingredients needed:

2 cups	grape juice, or fruit juice of your choice	500 mL
	1 pkg. unflavoured gelatin	

Utensils needed:

measuring cup

small saucepan or large glass measuring cup

wooden spoon

popsicle molds or small paper cups and wooden sticks

(adult help)

How to prepare:

1. Pour 1 cup (250 mL) juice into the saucepan (for stove-top cooking) or measuring cup (for microwave). Sprinkle the gelatin onto the surface of the juice and let it stand for 5 minutes.
2. Stove-top method: Heat and stir over medium heat until the mixture is very hot and the gelatin has dissolved. Microwave method: Cook on Medium for 3 minutes, stirring each minute, until mixture is hot and gelatin dissolves.
3. As soon as the gelatin dissolves, remove from heat and stir in the remaining cold juice.
4. Pour into molds or cups and put in freezer for 30 minutes. Insert sticks into the partially frozen popsicles, then return to freezer and leave until completely frozen.

Makes 4 to 6 jelly-sicles.

Chocolate Banana Pops

(adult supervision)

A frozen treat that's easy to make.

Ingredients needed:

½ cup   chopped semisweet or   125 mL
        milk chocolate

1 large banana

Utensils needed:

sharp knife and cutting board

measuring cup

small saucepan or microwave-safe bowl

wooden spoon

2 wooden sticks

table knife

small tray or plate covered with
waxed paper

plastic wrap

How to prepare:

1. Chop chocolate, then put in saucepan (for stove-top cooking) or bowl (for microwave cooking).
2. Stove-top method: Melt chocolate over low heat. Stir with a wooden spoon as chocolate melts. When melted, turn off stove and remove from heat. Microwave method: Melt chocolate on Medium for 1 to 2 minutes. Stir once or twice during melting.
3. Peel banana and cut in half. Push wooden sticks into the cut ends of each banana piece. Use the table knife to completely cover the banana with melted chocolate.
4. Put the chocolate-coated banana pieces on the waxed-paper-covered tray and place in the freezer for 1 hour.
5. After 1 hour, either wrap the banana pieces in plastic wrap and leave in the freezer, or eat right away.

Makes 2 servings.

VARIATION 1:
Coconut Banana Pops

Cut banana in half as above and push sticks into the cut end of each piece. Coat the banana pieces completely with plain or flavoured yogurt. Roll each piece in coconut and freeze as above.

VARIATION 2:
Granola Banana Pops

Coat the banana halves in yogurt as above, then roll in your favourite granola for an extra-crunchy treat. Freeze as above.

Ice Cream Sandwich

Make these ahead of time—they're easier to eat when they have been frozen.

Ingredients needed:

2 graham crackers or large cookies

1 scoop of your favourite ice cream

Utensils needed:

ice cream scoop

table knife

plastic wrap

(adult supervision)

How to prepare:

1. Spread slightly softened ice cream on one graham cracker or cookie, completely covering the cracker with ice cream.
2. Gently press the second cracker on top of the ice cream. Wrap in plastic wrap and freeze for 1 hour, or until firm.

Makes 1 sandwich.

VARIATION:
Roll the ice cream edges of your sandwich in granola, coconut, chopped nuts, or miniature chocolate chips before freezing.

8
Cookies, Squares, and Candies

Funny Face Cookies

(adult supervision)

Ingredients needed:

½ cup   peanut butter, jelly,   125 mL
or frosting

6 plain round cookies
or crackers

Decorations: coconut, grated carrot, raisins, small candies, dried fruit, coloured sugar, chocolate sprinkles

Utensils needed:

table knife

How to prepare:

1. Spread a thin layer of peanut butter, jelly, or frosting on each cookie or cracker.
2. Make funny faces on the cookies using whatever decorations you have available. Use coconut or grated carrot for hair, and raisins, small candies, or dried fruit for eyes, nose, mouth, and ears. Use coloured sugar or chocolate sprinkles for freckles.

Makes 6 funny faces.

Mud Pies

One child I know calls these "haystacks." Whatever you call them, they're great to eat!

Ingredients needed:

2 cups	sugar	500 mL
½ cup	milk	125 mL
½ cup	shortening or margarine	125 mL
5 tbsp.	cocoa	75 mL
1 tsp.	vanilla	5 mL
½ tsp.	salt	2 mL
3 cups	oatmeal	750 mL
1 cup	coconut	250 mL

Utensils needed:

measuring cups and spoons

large glass measuring cup or medium saucepan

wooden spoon

medium mixing bowl

2 spoons

cookie sheet

waxed paper

(adult help)

How to prepare:

1. Measure sugar, milk, shortening, cocoa, vanilla, and salt into the large glass measuring cup (if you plan to cook in the microwave) or a medium saucepan (if you plan to cook on the stove top). Stir to mix ingredients together.
2. Microwave method: Cook on High for 3 to 5 minutes, or until the shortening melts and the mixture boils. Stir twice during cooking.
   Stove-top method: Cook and stir over medium heat until shortening melts and mixture boils.
3. Remove from burner or microwave. Combine oatmeal and coconut in mixing bowl and add all at once to sugar mixture. Stir to mix well.
4. Drop spoonfuls of the mixture onto the waxed-paper-lined cookie sheet. Refrigerate or leave on counter until firm. Store in an airtight container in a cool place.

Makes about 40 cookies.

Granola Bars

Delicious lunch-box treats. Wrap and freeze individually for quick snacks.

Ingredients needed:

¾ cup	butter or margarine	175 mL
1 cup	brown sugar	250 mL
1 cup	raisins	250 mL
1 cup	chocolate chips	250 mL
4 cups	rolled oats	1 L
1 cup	chopped nuts	250 mL
¼ cup	oat bran	50 mL
¼ cup	sunflower seeds	50 mL
	2 eggs	

Utensils needed:

small saucepan

wooden spoon

measuring cups

large mixing bowl

small bowl and fork

13 x 9-inch (34 x 22 cm) baking pan, greased

(adult help)

How to prepare:

1. Measure butter and sugar into saucepan. Cook over low heat until butter melts and sugar is dissolved. Stir occasionally.
2. Measure remaining ingredients except eggs into a large bowl. Pour the melted butter mixture into the bowl and stir to mix all ingredients well. Beat the eggs in a small bowl with a fork, then mix the eggs into the other ingredients.
3. Press the mixture into the prepared baking pan. Bake in a preheated 300°F (150°C) oven for 15 minutes. Cool in the pan for 15 minutes before cutting into bars.

Makes 16 bars.

Chocolate Chip Cookie Squares

(adult help)

My friend Dyan brought a pan of these to a winter picnic. They taste just like chocolate chip cookies, but are much faster to make.

Ingredients needed:

⅔ cup	soft shortening	150 mL
½ cup	white sugar	125 mL
½ cup	brown sugar	125 mL
	1 egg	
1 tsp.	vanilla	5 mL
1½ cups	flour	375 mL
½ tsp.	baking soda	2 mL
½ tsp.	salt	2 mL
1 cup	chocolate chips	250 mL

Utensils needed:

measuring cups and spoons

large mixing bowl

wooden spoon

small mixing bowl

13 x 9-inch (34 x 22 cm) baking pan, greased

plastic wrap

How to prepare:

1. Cream shortening and both sugars in large mixing bowl. Add egg and vanilla and stir until well mixed.
2. Measure flour, baking soda, and salt into a small bowl and stir to mix well. Add this mixture to the sugar mixture and stir until well mixed. Stir in chocolate chips.
3. Press the dough evenly into the prepared baking pan. This will be easier if you cover the dough with plastic wrap and use your hands to press the dough into the pan. Bake in a preheated 375°F (190°C) oven for 20 minutes, or until brown and firm to the touch. Cool before cutting into squares.

Makes 36 squares.

Cereal Squares

Use any kind of cereal in these squares, but be sure not to change the total amount used.

Ingredients needed:

¼ cup	margarine	50 mL
	40 marshmallows	
5 cups	mixed dry cereals	1.25 L
½ cup	gumdrops, or chopped candied or dried fruit (optional)	125 mL

Utensils needed:

measuring cups

large saucepan or large glass measuring cup

wooden spoon

9-inch (22 cm) square baking pan, greased

rubber spatula

bowl of cold water

sharp knife

(adult help)

How to prepare:

1. Measure margarine and marshmallows into large saucepan (if you are going to cook on the stove top) or glass measuring cup (if you are going to use a microwave).
2. Stove-top method: Cook and stir margarine and marshmallows in a large saucepan over low heat until both ingredients are melted. Microwave method: Microwave measuring cup containing margarine and marshmallows on High for 2 to 3 minutes, stirring every minute, until melted.
3. Stir in remaining ingredients. Pour mixture into the baking pan and press down firmly using a wet rubber spatula or your clean, wet hands. (The water keeps the marshmallow mixture from sticking to the spatula or your hands.)
4. Cut into squares when cool and firm.

Makes 25 squares.

Peanut Butter Crunchies

My friend Fiona calls these "Rickety Uncles." Isn't that a great name for these lopsided treats?

Ingredients needed:

⅔ cup	corn syrup	150 mL
⅔ cup	peanut butter	150 mL
2 cups	cornflakes	500 mL
2 cups	crisped rice cereal	500 mL

Utensils needed:

measuring cups

large glass measuring cup or medium saucepan

wooden spoon

spoons

cookie sheet

waxed paper

(adult help)

How to prepare:

1. Measure corn syrup and peanut butter into glass measuring cup (if you are using a microwave) or saucepan (if you are cooking on the stove top).
2. Microwave method: Microwave on Medium until mixture is smooth and quite hot, about 3 minutes. Stir twice during cooking.
   Stove-top method: Cook and stir over low heat until mixture is smooth and hot.
3. Add cereals to peanut butter mixture and stir to blend well.
4. Drop mixture by spoonfuls onto waxed-paper-covered cookie sheet. Serve when cool and firm.

Makes 4 to 5 dozen.

Peanut Butter Balls

(adult supervision)

These taste so good that you'll forget they're good for you!

Ingredients needed:

½ cup	peanut butter	125 mL
2 tbsp.	milk powder	25 mL
1 tbsp.	liquid honey	15 mL
¼ cup	wheat germ	50 mL
¼ cup	coconut	50 mL
¼ cup	chopped peanuts	50 mL
½ cup	graham cracker crumbs	125 mL

Utensils needed:

mixing bowl and wooden spoon

measuring cups and spoons

spoon

small bowl

waxed paper

cookie sheet

How to prepare:

1. Mix together in a bowl the peanut butter, milk powder, honey, and wheat germ. Stir in coconut and peanuts.
2. Take a spoonful of the dough and roll into a small ball with your (clean) hands.
3. Put crumbs in a small bowl and coat the peanut butter balls in the crumbs. Place balls on a waxed-paper-covered cookie sheet and refrigerate until firm.

Makes about 2 dozen.

Peanut Butter Candy Creams

A special occasion treat to share with friends.

Ingredients needed:

¼ cup	icing sugar	50 mL
1 cup	chocolate chips	250 mL
½ cup	sweetened condensed milk	125 mL
1 cup	peanut butter	250 mL
	chocolate sprinkles or chopped nuts	

Utensils needed:

mixing bowl and wooden spoon

measuring cups

rubber spatula

spoon

small bowl

cookie sheet

waxed paper

(adult supervision)

How to prepare:

1. Stir icing sugar and chocolate chips together in mixing bowl. Blend in sweetened condensed milk, then stir in peanut butter.
2. Take a small spoonful of the dough and shape it into a ball using your (clean) hands.
3. Put the sprinkles or nuts in a small bowl and roll the balls in whichever coating you have chosen.
4. Put finished balls on a waxed-paper-lined cookie sheet and refrigerate until firm.

Makes about 3 dozen.

Hand Cookies

Decorate to look like hands, then give your friends and relatives a "hand" as a gift!

Ingredients needed:

⅔ cup	shortening	150 mL
¾ cup	sugar	175 mL
1 tsp.	vanilla	5 mL
	1 egg	
4 tsp.	milk	20 mL
2 cups	flour	500 mL
1½ tsp.	baking powder	7 mL
¼ tsp.	salt	1 mL
	coloured icing	
	candy decorations	

Utensils needed:

large, medium, and small mixing bowls

measuring cups and spoons

wooden spoon

plastic wrap

rolling pin

table knife

greased cookie sheet

metal spatula

decorating bag

(adult help)

How to prepare:

1. In a large mixing bowl, cream together the shortening and sugar. Stir in vanilla. Break the egg into a small bowl and remove any shell bits that may have fallen in. Stir the egg into the shortening mixture. Add the milk and mix well.
2. In a medium mixing bowl stir together the flour, baking powder, and salt. Blend this dry mixture into the shortening mixture in the large bowl. Shape the dough into a ball, wrap in plastic wrap and refrigerate for 1 hour.
3. Preheat oven to 375°F (190°C).
4. Roll chilled dough on a lightly floured surface to ¼-inch (6 mm) thick. Put your (clean) hand on the dough and use a dull table knife to cut out a "cookie hand" by tracing around your own hand. Carefully lift onto greased cookie sheet using a metal spatula. Cut out more hands, then make smaller cookies with the remaining dough.
5. Bake cookies for 8 to 10 minutes, or until cookies are light brown and firm to the touch. Cool the cookies on the

cookie sheet—they will break if you try to lift them while they are warm.

6. Use coloured icing and candy decorations to decorate cooled cookie hands with rings, watches, bracelets, fingernails, or your name. Be creative!

Makes about 12 cookies.

Microwave Peanut Butter S'mores

(adult help)

When S'mores were first invented, they were made with marshmallows roasted over a campfire (still a good way to make them!). This microwave version lets you enjoy S'mores anytime.

Ingredients needed:

peanut butter

8 graham crackers

a few chocolate chips

2 marshmallows

Utensils needed:

table knife

microwave-safe or paper plate

How to prepare:

1. Spread a thin layer of peanut butter on 4 graham crackers. Stick a few chocolate chips on the peanut butter. Put the crackers on the plate. Cut marshmallows in half and press one marshmallow half on top of the chocolate chips, cut side down.
2. Microwave on High for 1 minute, or until the marshmallow becomes soft.
3. Remove from microwave, then place a graham cracker on top of each marshmallow half. Eat the S'mores while they are warm.

Makes 4 servings.

Index